Sport for Sport:
Theoretical
and Practical Insights
into Sports Development

Editors
**Spencer Harris, Barbara Bell,
Andrew Adams and Chris Mackintosh**

LSA

LSA Publication No. 117

Sport for Sport: Theoretical and Practical Insights
into Sports Development

First published in 2012 by
Leisure Studies Association
The Chelsea School
University of Brighton
Eastbourne BN20 7SP (UK)

A catalogue record for this book
is available from the British Library.

ISBN:
978 1 905369 28 7

Cover painting by kind permission of Sandra Bailey Brazier
Cover design and page layout Myrene L. McFee

Printed and bound by CPI Group (UK) Ltd, Croydon, CR0 4YY

Contents

ABOUT THE CONTRIBUTORS

Dr. Andrew Adams is a senior lecturer in the Faculty of Business, Sport and Enterprise at Southampton Solent University. He is course leader for sport coaching and development and leads the faculty's sport research. Andrew's research interests include sport and social capital, human rights in sport and the role of the voluntary sports clubs in the promotion of social policy.

Dr. Aaron Beacom has taught at University College Plymouth St. Mark and St John since 2002 where he is now Reader in sport and international relations and MA Programme Leader. He has a Ph.D. in Politics (University of Exeter). He is co-editor of *Sport and International Development* (Palgrave 2009). Other recent publications include an authored paper in the *European Sports Management Quarterly* (2007) and co-authored chapters in Girginov(ed) (2008) *Management of Sports Development* and Houlihan and Green (eds) (2011) *Routledge Handbook of Sports Development*. His current research interest concerns emerging diplomatic discourses as they relate to Olympic and Paralympic sport.

Dr. Barbara Bell Currently Senior Lecturer at Manchester Metropolitan University, teaching at Undergraduate and Postgraduate levels in Sport Development and supervising several students in research degrees. Since gaining her PhD at Loughborough in 2005, her research has focused on youth sport and policy evaluation in sport development, more recently with a focus on women's football, events and event legacy in sporting outcomes. Barbara started her academic career after 10 years in community sport and leisure management. She has presented and published papers and book chapters relating to social sport marketing, Champion Coaching and youth sports and has an interest in multi-disciplinary approaches and social realist methodology. An active member of the ESDN and LSA, Barbara has contributed to several LSA volumes. Her book *Sport Studies* was published by Learning Matters in 2009.

Stuart Bonner is a senior lecturer in Physical Education, Sport Coaching and Development at Sheffield Hallam University. Stuart has a BA in Human Movement Studies and has qualified teacher status in Physical Education. Following several years teaching in secondary education in Nottingham, Stuart moved to Sheffield Hallam University where his teaching areas include sport coaching and leadership, games activities in PE and youth sport and alternative physical activities. Stuart is also an LTA senior performance tennis coach.

Steve Bullough is a research fellow at the Sport Industry Research Centre at Sheffield Hallam University. Steve has a BSc in Sport Management and an MSc in Organisational Development and Consultancy and his research interests span across a range of research projects. His recent work has focussed particularly on the monitoring and evaluation of policy and practice for both individual sports and whole programmes such as Sport Unlimited and Everyday Swim. Steve's other areas of interest are the economics of sport, sport participation and major events.

Dr. Jonathan Grix, Senior Lecturer in Sport Policy and Politics, is one of only a few academics from a politics background to turn his attention to the study of sport. His research interests include sport policy, the politics of sport, sporting mega events and their legacies, elite sport development and East German sport, in particular as a model for contemporary sport systems. On the latter, Grix has recently produced — with Professor Mike Dennis — the first English language study of East Germany drawing on original German archival documents, entitled *Sport Under Communism: Behind the East German 'Miracle'*, published by Palgrave (2012).

Spencer Harris is currently an Assistant Professor in the Department of Human Performance and Physical Education at Adams State College in Colorado, USA. His previous experience includes 16 years in community sports development, working as a Sport Development Manager at Crawley Borough Council; as Head of Performance for Sport England East; and spending a year in Arua, Uganda as a Project Coordinator for Right to Play. In addition, he worked as a Senior Lecturer in Sports Development at the University of Hertfordshire 2008–11. Spencer's publications include work on voluntary sport and sport policy. He is currently in the final year of his Ph.D. which is focused on analysing the relationship between National Governing Bodies of Sport and County Sport Partnerships in the implementation of increased participation in community sport.

Gemma Hart is a research fellow at the Sport Industry Research Centre, Sheffield Hallam University. Gemma's research interests focus on evaluating interventions aimed at encouraging more young people to participate in physical activity. Gemma also has a strong interest in participation in physical activity by 16–19 year olds, an age group where historically there is significant drop out in participation. Gemma has recently undertaken analysis of the Active People data sets analysing where drop out in participation occurs amongst 16–19 year olds. Gemma recently presented the findings from this research at the European Association for Sport Management conference in Prague.

Dr. Hazel Hartley is a Principal Lecturer in the Carnegie Faculty, Leeds Metropolitan University. She has taught sport law and ethics for 30 years and is the course leader of the MA Sport, Law and Society. Her research interests are around corporate liability and leadership in health and safety, disasters and the law. Over the last twenty years her research activism has contributed to various consultations, legal investigations/inquiries, and collaborative campaigns for legal reform. Her publications include *Sport, Physical Recreation and the Law* (Routledge 2009) and *Exploring Sport and Leisure Disasters* (Cavendish-Routledge, 2001).

Kevin Hylton is Professor of Social Sciences in Sport, Leisure and PE, Carnegie Faculty, Leeds Metropolitan University, UK. Kevin's research interests focus on the development of Critical Race Theory (CRT), diversity, equity and inclusion in sport, leisure and PE. Kevin has been heavily involved in community sports development and has worked with marginalised groups and representative bodies in different settings. Kevin's publications include *Sports Development: Policy, Process and Practice* (2001; 2008, Hylton, forthcoming 2012); and *'Race' and Sport: Critical Race Theory* (Routledge, 2009).

Chris Mackintosh worked at the Sports Council for Wales policy evaluation unit before taking up his first lectureship at Edge Hill University. He also worked for two years as a management consultant in sports development for clients including Sport England, Rugby Football League and a number of local authorities on regional strategies, lottery bids and research projects. He is now a senior lecturer in sports development at Nottingham Trent University where his current research interests include community sports development, partnership working and sports role in crime prevention and social inclusion. Recently he was appointed as an academic advisor to Street Games UK and as a research consultant to the English Table Tennis Association on their outdoor table tennis initiative evaluation. He has been a frequent contributor to *PE and Sport Today*, *Recreation* and *Inform* (ISPAL magazine). He was the founder of the European Sports Development Network (ESDN) in October 2008 and organiser of the inaugural symposium.

Richard Moore is a research fellow at the Sport Industry Research Centre at Sheffield Hallam University with a BA in Journalism and an MSc in Sport and Recreation Management. His main research focus is the evaluation of sport or leisure programmes. Richard has recently worked on a variety of projects including a national coaching workforce study on behalf of Sport Northern Ireland and the evaluation of three green exercise programmes for Natural England. Richard has played a significant role in monitoring and evaluating the Sport Unlimited programme on behalf of Sport England.

Dr. Lesley Phillpots is a lecturer in physical education and sports policy in the School of Education at the University of Birmingham, UK. She teaches on a range of under- and post-graduate courses and is Programme Co-ordinator for the BA Sport, PE and Coaching Science degree. Her research interests focus primarily upon policy for sport, school sport and physical education. She has recently written book chapters on youth sport development in the UK and partnership approaches to the delivery of youth sport and physical education. She is currently writing and publishing a range of articles that focus on the governance of sport, the work of County Sport Partnerships, the PE & Sport Strategy for Young People (PESSYP) and the life histories of female PGA golf teaching professionals. Lesley has published work in *Public Policy and Administration* and the *International Review for the Sociology of Sport*. She is also co-editing (with Dr Jonathan Grix) *Understanding UK Sport Policy: A Comparative Context*, Routledge, forthcoming) and a Special Issue for the *International Journal for Sport Policy*.

Dr. Alex Stewart is with the Department of PE & Sport Studies at the University of Bedfordshire. Alex's central research interests lie in the critical investigation of sport through insider ethnographic methodology and socio-logical, cultural and social-psychological theory. His academic interests and teaching competences also take in the following related areas: the social-isation process into and through sport; sport and social inequalities of class, gender, 'race'; sporting subcultures; and sport development in rela-tion to aspects of sport, culture and embodiment; social inclusion/ exclusion; youth development; crime reduction and education

Leona Trimble is Principal Lecturer and Division Leader for Sport Coach-ing and Development at the University of Central Lancashire. Areas of teaching and research include sport and community capacity building, volunteering, club development, sports development policy and delivery and international sports development. Leona began her career in health club management before working as a sports development officer for the Chesh-ire & Warrington Sports Partnership focusing on Active Sports club develop-ment and organising the Cheshire Youth Games. Leona has worked in higher education for eight years.

SPORT FOR SPORT: THEORETICAL AND PRACTICAL INSIGHTS INTO SPORTS DEVELOPMENT — EDITORS' INTRODUCTION

Spencer Harris, Barbara Bell, Andrew Adams and Christopher Mackintosh

The papers presented in this volume have been developed from original presentations at a one-day symposium held in September 2010. The symposium was a collaborative initiative between ESDN and Leisure Studies Association and was hosted by the University of Hertfordshire. The symposium brought together academics and practitioners with the aim of sharing thoughts, ideas and research about sports development as well as identifying and discussing challenges and further research questions which confront the future of sports development.

All of the papers in this collection are concerned with identifying and developing theoretical and conceptual insights, from a variety of academic fields, into UK-based sports development policy and practice. The symposium itself came at a time when policy towards the development of sport in England was taking a turn away from what has been termed 'sport for good' to 'sport for sport'. This situation followed a brief power struggle between ministers within the UK Department of Culture, Media and Sport and the chairman of Sport England, resulting in the then sports minister Gerry Sutcliffe announcing in 2008 a shift from promoting physical activity to a focus on sport for sport (Collins, 2010). This significant change of strategic direction for sport in England has also been mirrored internationally as global economic and financial pressures have ensured that state-funded services have become prone to greater scrutiny in terms of efficiency and effectiveness. This level of scrutiny has arguably placed greater pressure on the validity of state support for the use of sport as a tool of development. Certainly in the UK, the London Olympics gaze and the installation of a new national government have contributed to a shift in sports development from inclusion-related aspirations to those more bluntly concerned with participation targets and medal winning potential.

This backdrop of legitimacy, viability and coherence to and of sport development sets the tone for many of the presentations at the symposium and certainly connects the papers presented in this volume. The challenge of the symposium to bring academic and practitioners together is also reflected in the chapters presented here. Each brings elements of translation from theory to practice and should allow not only for reflection on professional practice, but also for closer synergies between academics and practitioners. In so doing, this volume addresses a concern voiced by Barrie Houlihan (2011) that that academics are not doing enough to narrow the gap between researchers and research users. This volume makes a significant contribution to that agenda.

In the first chapter **Kevin Hylton and Hazel Hartley** discuss sports development as a profession. They argue that whilst sports development may claim to be a profession, on closer inspection it fails to meet a number of criteria commonly attached to professions — for example a common or agreed definition, a unifying body, any enforceable entry requirements, an ethical code, and has no powers of exclusion or restrictions of practice. They concede that sports development may be moving toward professional status, but that a number of challenges must be addressed by the Institute of the Management of Sport and Physical Activity (IMSPA) to fully galvanise sports development as full and proper professional entity.

Lesley Philpott and Jonathan Grix use the growing body of governance literature to explore the increasing politicisation of physical education (PE) and youth sport policy with a focus on the School Club Links work strand of the UK Government's 'Physical Education and Sport Strategy for Young People' (PESSYP). They reflect on the idea of 'new' governance arrangements for policy delivery and implementation, where the desire is the apparent erosion of central government power in favour of more localised partnerships and networks. They argue that whilst the PE and youth sport policy sector may exhibit 'new' governance characteristics, Government intervention and centralised state control permeates all levels of Physical Education and youth sport policy delivery and implementation.

School sport is analysed further with **Steve Bullough, Gemma Hart, Richard Moore and Stuart Bonner** presenting a number of key issues emanating from their evaluation of the Sport Unlimited programme. In their examination they emphasise the importance of the 'student voice' in designing and developing school-based sports programmes and, through this, the recognition of alternative physical activities as a key feature of the county-based Sports Unlimited delivery plans.

Reflecting on the process of socialisation, **Alex Stewart** provides an insider account of elite and amateur male boxing subculture. His research explores the relationship between the cultural production of amateur boxing and the aims of sports development as a process of personal and social change. His paper demonstrates the necessity to contest the nature, boundaries and definitions of the field, and provides an example of the utility of sociological theory to sports development practice.

Aaron Beacom focuses on the relationship between bid city and state in the quest to host major events. In particular, his paper examines the tension between the city and state as stakeholders in the bidding for Olympic and Paralympic Games and argues that recent scholarly work in multi-stakeholder diplomacy can provide a useful lens through which to view the dynamics of state and sub-state diplomacy in relation to the Olympic and Paralympic Games.

Against a backdrop of considerable policy change and emphasis on traditional (NGBs) and new (CSP) structures, **Chris Mackintosh** examines the shifting dynamics of public sector sports development and sets out to identify the range and nature of challenges that face public sector sports development practitioners. In particular the research points to an ongoing tension between pure sports development and sport-for-development objectives, the challenge posed by the realities of evidence-based practice, and the need for sports development to continually adapt, create and/or integrate with new models of delivery.

Leona Trimble investigates the issue of women's leadership though a case study involving a coaching project in South Africa. She identifies a number of issues including female empowerment, local cultural sensitivities and leadership development. The paper examines some of the possibilities of sport and policy aimed at using sport as an agent of change and presents some critical discussion of the limitations and fallibility of such approaches.

The aspiration attached to this publication is to develop and share a broader knowledge and wider appreciation of sports development and to ensure that sport development practice is informed by insightful, innovative and critical thought. To this end we hope that the publication is interesting, thought-provoking and stimulates further ideas and research questions to broaden our understanding of the field.

References

Collins, M. (2010) 'From "sport for good" to "sport for sport's sake" — not a good move for sports development in England?', *International Journal of Sport Policy* Vol. 2, No. 3: pp. 367–379.
Houlihan, B. (2011) 'Leisure studies: Influential as well as interesting?', Keynote presentation to Leisure Studies Association Conference, Southampton Solent University, July 5–7, 2011.

**Spencer Harris, Barbara Bell, Andrew Adams
    and Christopher Mackintosh**
September, 2011

SPORTS DEVELOPMENT:
A PROFESSION IN WAITING...?

Kevin Hylton and Hazel J. Hartley

Carnegie Faculty, Leeds Metropolitan University

Introduction

This chapter captures some of the current debates in sports development concerning the nature of its claims to be recognised as a profession. It emerges from reflections on the nature and purpose of sports development courses in higher education, the perceptions of students on their 'profession', and employer views of student readiness for the field. Though what constitutes a profession is ultimately not uncontested, it is clear from literature in the sociology of the professions that there is much agreement on the fundamental parallels in modern professions. Questions remain about whether sports development is a profession; whether it should be a profession; and if it is a profession, what qualifies this assessment. The chapter also reflects on sport's latest bid for professional recognition through the Chartered Institute of Sport[1] manifesto, and its establishment, which adds to the richness of the current debates on a sports development profession framework.

A common way of viewing sports development as a profession is from an experiential perspective, which one might say is a more likely lens adopted by its practitioners. Sports development is a recent phenomenon whose construction has been the result of many factors that include practice, policy and theory. For many, sports development is regarded as a profession of *identity*. A critical analysis of sports development as a profession requires more than this implicit acceptance, which is where we now turn.

Part of the motivation for exploring whether there is a sports development profession was instigated after a systematic review of the literature on Black and Minority Ethnic (BME) Communities in sport and physical recreation by the Carnegie Research Institute[2] that drew attention to some of the baffling anomalies in sports development policy and practice. These peculiarities are symptomatic of sports development over the years (Long, Hylton *et al.*, 2009). In conducting the review this report was not just concerned with what is, but how opportunities might be extended and improved for BME groups. The challenge, then, was to establish what works for whom in what circumstances and how particular programmes work. The goal was to inform policy and practice. What was of particular interest was not only the way simple successful community sport ideas were lauded but also how those paid to manage in sport organizations have demonstrated an inability to systematically train their workers to monitor, evaluate and disseminate good practice. This is indicative of a field that does not meticulously educate its professionals in terms of its history and competencies, nor conduct, as a matter of professional standards, any compulsory continuing professional development (CPD).

The fundamentals of sports development are constantly being fractured or lost as great ideas, practices, and generations of professionals in sports development have to learn and relearn on the job due to the random entry routes into the 'profession'. Hence it is likely that we will read more expensive research or evaluations about 'new techniques' where good practice has been demonstrated in sports development such as out-reach work, empowering communities, sustainable resourcing, joined-up thinking, and partnership working ... old wine in new bottles. These ideas need to move on further than when first mooted in earlier years. A cursory comparison of community sport reports from the 1980s and the 2000s illustrates this haphazard development of theory, policy and practice in 'sports development'. As a result, knowledge development is hampered by the stymied flow of ideas and issues, with the coherence of education affected across the sector. For example the Active Communities (Sport England, 2002: p. 10) evaluation argued that it was "a courageous programme which attempts to address deep-seated structural imbalances in sport" and in society generally; similar sentiments were written in the Action Sport evaluation in the 1980s by Rigg (1986).

Background context of sports development in England

In the early days of local authority sport through the 1960s and 1970s many of those in positions of responsibility often had a PE/teaching background. PE teaching was a commonly recognised professional education in sport beyond gaining governing body coaching awards. Over the years sports developers have emerged, due to (a) the explosion in the1970s of recreation facilities and Sports Council campaigns, (b) the emphasis on community sport development in the 1980s, and (c) in the emergence of more coherent sports strategies from the 1990s onwards. More recently professional bodies like NASD (National Association of Sports Development) and ISPAL (Institute for Sport, Parks and Leisure) have emerged to try and galvanise a relatively disparate group of sport developers into a recognisable force for public good, hopefully with their influence being felt in political circles at all levels. As part of this, there have also been moves by ISPAL to establish national occupational standards for sports development.

In the 1990s there was a small number of university courses with sports development in their title. Now there is a plethora of sports development courses on UCAS's books for a 2011 start, including related sport studies courses with a combination of core and electives with a sports development focus. There was no coherent literature on sports development, and the field was even less defined than it is now. In 2001 we were involved in a text that would draw core learning materials and contexts together to enhance and make visible a multi-disciplinary academic field that did not previously exist with a sports development focus (Hylton, Bramham *et al.*, 2001; Hylton and Bramham, 2008). Using what C. Wright Mills called *the sociological imagination*, the edited collection set about encapsulating what sports development meant from a number of complementary disciplinary fields. This was underpinned by philosophical perspectives on sports development as a contested concept. This and subsequent sports development texts had the twin outcomes of focusing the emergent field for academics while giving students and practitioners a starting point for their critical practice (Collins and Kay, 2003; Girginov, 2008; Houlihan and Green, 2010; Houlihan and White, 2002).

Defining the field

Returning to the duplication of ideas and 'Eureka moments', disciplines recognised as professions (or even semi-professions) tend to share their core ideas and practices — 'social work', 'law', 'accounting', 'teaching' — so that good practice is shared, critiqued and developed from positions of strength. Ethical and philosophical approaches are established, and guides put in place to underpin them; standards are set and reached before progression into the sector, and benchmarks of good practice are readily available in a variety of contexts. For sports development there are no guarantees that having statutory guidelines will improve practice, though it is more likely that basic levels of competence and standards will be in place and expected across the sector and beyond if they are implemented.

Part of the rationale for this chapter came out of concerns regarding how the 'profession' has developed. Our interest emerged from planning a study on a) how sports development students view their career aspirations and the 'profession' and b) how practitioners view student readiness for the 'profession'. Before beginning this study we were compelled to turn to the focus of this chapter and more fundamental matters: *whether sports development is indeed a profession and if so what makes it one*. We view with caution sports development as a *profession* mainly because of our history and connections with it, and not because we think it is not populated by committed *professionals*.

Hylton has argued elsewhere that sports development must be "used to describe processes, policies and practices that form an integral feature of the work involved in providing sporting opportunities" (Hylton *et al.*, 2001; 2008: p. 1). Sports development should also be thought of as comprehensive inclusive processes, which engage the broadest spectrum of policy makers, agencies, organisations, practitioners and participants. This is mainly because for students of sports development a description of disparate fields needs to be wide-ranging and inclusive. On the face of it, academics have been able to theorise sports development well, establishing a full range of academic courses from college diplomas through to PhDs and producing sports development graduates on 142 degree courses in the UK each year (UCAS).

Theorising sports development has contributed to the analysis of contemporary and current policies that have influenced the planning and delivery of sport in its broadest sense. Similarly the critical lenses utilised in the study of sports development have been systematic in unpacking power relations and issues that cannot be ignored in establishing a fuller understanding of sport's place in social relations. For academics with a broad view of education, their sports development courses can be about deep learning, reflexivity, and the development of independent freethinking. Such graduates are able to apply these skills to a range of professional contexts in sport, leisure or beyond in sectors such as retail, human resources, or management.

The debate here is complex because it involves claims made by professionals in sport that there is a sports development 'profession'. Academics and practitioners are often ambiguous about 'sports development' as a profession. In addition to having a governing body, a sports development profession must be to clarify core competencies, knowledge and critiques. These parameters must be established at different levels otherwise core professional standards cannot be attained.

In this chapter we are writing to encourage sports development practitioners to be critical and accepting of what is necessary to consider in structuring a profession. For many, the simplest questions that first year undergraduates are likely to ask requires much more thought than has been explicitly documented in academic or professional circles to date. For example:

- How does one access 'the profession' at different levels?
- What qualifications are needed to get a good job?
- What qualifications are needed for CPD?
- How much and what sort of experience does one need to get in?
- What is a good starting salary for a new sports development professional?
- What is a traditional career path in this sports development profession?
- What sort of job should I expect to be doing in ten or fifteen years?

What is a profession?

Notions of a profession are contested and are regarded in contemporary literature as 'a process of an interacting network of institutions and people, not a checklist of attributes" (Khurana, 2010: p. 1). Professions themselves may also, at an operational level, develop further specialist groups and may be subject to rationalisation, re-stratification or re-professionalisation (see, for example, Broadbent *et al.*, 1997; Becher, 1999; Brock *et al.*, 1999; Pickard, 2009). There is however, a range of literature that attempts to articulate or identify the nature of a profession. Williams (1998: 18) suggests that to be a profession, a discipline should have:

> ... a defined scope, stating the profession's purpose and goals, qualifications for education, experience and professional development, a code of conduct to guide what should or should not, be done under given circumstances, recognised certification that requires maintenance and standards that are consistent with other peer groups.

The Australian Council of Professions (2004: p. 1) defined a profession as:

> ... a disciplined group of individuals who adhere to ethical standards and uphold themselves to and are accepted by, the

public as possessing special knowledge and skills, in a widely recognised body of learning derived from research, education and training at a high level, and who are prepared to exercise this knowledge and these skills in the interest of others. Inherent in this definition is the concept that the responsibility for the welfare, health and safety of the community shall take precedence over other considerations.

Cruess *et al.* (2004: p. 75) also identify a profession as "an occupation whose core element is work based on mastery of a complex body of knowledge and skills" where science, learning or art is "used in the service of others"and members are "governed by a code of ethics" where members "profess a commitment to competence, integrity and morality, altruism and the promotion of the public good within their domain". There is some kind of "social contract between a profession and society" which grants the profession a "monopoly over the use of its knowledge base" as well as autonomy and "the privilege of self-regulation" (Cruess *et al.*, 2004: p. 75). Earlier work by Burbules and Densmore (1991) identifies a profession in terms of autonomy and:

> ... a clearly defined, highly developed, specialized and theoretical knowledge base, control of training, certification and licensing of new entrants; self-governing and self-policing authority, especially with regard to professional ethics and members show a commitment to public service.

Established professions include medicine, dentistry, architecture, law, pharmacy, engineering, surveying and accountancy. Occupations which have debated the possibility, desirability or challenges of becoming a profession include management, sport management, sports coaching, executive coaching, and public relations (for example Duffy, 2009; Duffy *et al.*, 2010; Edwards, 2006; Hawkins, 2008; Mills, 1994; Reed and Anthony, 1992; Rostrok, 2009; Smith and Westerbeek 2004; Soucie, 1994). Members of a profession who have some degree of exclusivity, through restricted membership and a monopoly on providing a particular public service, enjoy a range of privileges. They merit social and, more importantly, legal recognition, which legitimizes their authority and autonomy, normally work full-time and are paid a salary commensurate with a particular level or role in that profession (Lindop, 1982; Warrior, 2002; Wilensky, 1964; Sockett, 1985). Such exclusivity and restrictive membership can attract criticism in sociology of the professions in the areas of power, diversity, access in training, career development and exclusionary sub-cultures (e.g. Edwards, 2006; Kennedy, 1992; Sommerlad, 2003, 2009).

Professions are also characterized by a high degree of skill, drawing on intellectual and specialised knowledge and expertise (Barber, 1965; Larson, 1997; Krejsler, 2005; Vollmer and Mills, 1966). Developing expected levels of knowledge and competence usually involves a higher qualification like a university degree. These awards are often followed by a post-graduate qualification and lengthy, expensive, and supervised training, both generic and in recognised specialities, as in medicine, surgery and law. The profession will normally set requirements for certain areas to be included in university undergraduate degrees and post-graduate courses — for example law, medicine, accountancy, and teaching. In order to remain licensed to practice, members of a profession are expected to maintain appropriate standards and keep up-to-date through a range of recognised continuous professional development courses (CPD), with so many points per seminar/course being required by the professional body (Williams, 1998). They also have to understand, follow and apply an ethical code of practice framed within and regulated by the profession (Larson, 1997). Professional Codes of Ethics are often based on deontology principles and virtue ethics (Hartley and Robinson, 2006). Simply having a code of ethics is not sufficient. The ability of a professional to make difficult ethical decisions with independence and autonomy, drawing on intellectual, research and policy domains, is often tested in the face of considerable, conflicting pressures in the workplace.

A professional body has the power to temporarily suspend and/ or expel a member from the profession (Barker, 2010; Perkin, 1985; Warrior, 2002). This requires considerable authority, expertise, significant resources and a degree of impartiality and independence from the other functions of a professional body. Consider the differing roles of the British Medical Association and the General Medical Council, as well as the costs to medical professionals, of member services such as the Medical Defence Union. A profession is thought to have a "crucial social function" doing something for society, providing a recognised service to the public or clients, often personal and confidential (Sockett, 1985, cited Warrior, 2002: p. 58; Barker, 2010).

Being a member of a profession is often associated with an altruistic attitude, a concern for public welfare, personal responsibility, commitment, and intrinsic values (Lindop, 1982; Patton, 1994; Smith and Westerbeek, 2004; Vollmer and Mills, 1966; Warrior, 2002). It is assumed that the public have a certain degree of trust in a profession, although this can change in different eras and contexts. Tobin (2004: p. 62) analysed efforts by the Institute of Public Relations to seek Royal Chartered status and noted that the "low levels of public trust" in "businesses, institutions and government" is "more than a passing trend". There is "no quick fix associated with building trust" particularly considering the "heritage" of public relations, "underlying motivations of PR campaigns or the business models employed, trust may never be wholly achievable" (Tobin, 2004: p. 63). Within the UK, however, the Institute of Public Relations' (IPR) move to "chartered status, demonstrates, as a minimum, the PR sector's intent to operate fairly and professionally" (Tobin, 2004: p. 63).

Smith and Westerbeek (2004: p. 38) argue that the ideology underpinning professionalism seems to have changed little along the way, but observe that in sport management in Australia there is "increased emphasis on commerce, commodification, sponsorship and entertainment, demanding specific professional preparation". They question the "assumption that students in sport management are entering a profession" (Smith and Westerbeek, 2004: p. 38). Durkheim (1957) viewed a profession as "the predominant vehicle for self-interest to be withheld in favour of the needs of community and society" where education of such professionals would be "focused on training individuals to sublimate their own importance and best interests in favour of the community" (Durkheim, 1957, cited Smith and Westerbeek, 2004: p. 41). Others believe that professionals are "no more altruistic than business people or any other profit-seeking workers" (Parsons, 1938, cited Smith and Westerbeek, 2004: 41).

Although more contemporary literature regards the notion of a profession as "a process of an interacting network of institutions and people, not a checklist of attributes" (Khurana, 2010: p. 1), the notion of an interacting network may actually be more appealing to sports development. A profession is recognised as a high level occupation, with a complex body of specialised knowledge and skills, usually involving lengthy and expensive post-graduate training and career development. It has autonomy, privilege, a degree of exclusivity and self-regulation, although this may attract criticism around access, power, diversity and exclusionary practices. It usually involves a licence to practice, a code of ethics and the power to suspend or expel a member. A profession normally involves the provision of a legally recognised public service and is associated with an altruistic attitude, personal responsibility and intrinsic values.

A profession in waiting?

The notion of "a professional" is different to "being professional" or professionalising a field. Hargreaves (2000: p. 152) said of his work on professionalism in teaching:

> Ask teachers what it means to be professional and they will usually refer to two things. First they will talk about *being* professional...teachers will also talk about *being a* professional. [emphasis added]

It could also be argued that a similar response would be forthcoming from speaking to practitioners in sports development. Krejsler (2005) also distinguishes between being in a profession and being professional. Being professional, he argues, is attitudinal in regard to personal commitment, self-motivation, pride in standards of work, affiliation with colleagues, and a wish for personal or professional autonomy. In other words sports development could be described as a profession of identity, without being a profession. Hargreaves (2000) goes on to argue that when teachers talk about being professional they are referring to qualitative and ethical aspects of their performance in the role of teacher. This reference to professionalism refers to the quality of what actors do at work, their conduct, and standards that guide them. Being a *professional* enables people to see themselves as others see them.

Thinking through the criteria used to describe a profession, can sports development be regarded as a profession? Do those who work in sports development have a degree of exclusivity, restricted/selective membership and a monopoly on providing a public service, which their association markets? Everyone who works in sports development could be said to contribute to a public service, a social good, although there is no formal association as yet which can restrict members or which actively markets that service. The proposed Chartered Institute of Sport, ISPAL and Institute of Sport and Recreation Management (ISRM) (2009) tried to address some of these needs. In relation to setting standards and a core body of knowledge associated with a profession, ISPAL in association with SkillsActive) has already made progress with both national occupational standards (NOS) and the implementation of a system of recognising or endorsing university degrees in sports development in the UK.

The merger of ISRM and ISPAL to form the Institute for the Management of Sport and Physical Activity (IMSPA) appears to be a significant step towards professional status[3]. Since ISPAL is one of the founding organisations of the Chartered Institute of Sport, the area of sports development will have to address the challenge of compatibility with established professions such as medicine and law, which clearly develop specialist knowledge and skills beyond an undergraduate degree with clear post-graduate routes towards specialist roles, with associated salaries. This is not explicit in the manifesto, nor is there any evidence of clearly articulated and recognised CPD routes for members to maintain their certification or license. At present there is no sports development association for members that has the resources, impartiality and authority, like the General Medical Council, to suspend and/or expel a member. Even if sports development was part of the proposed Chartered Institute of Sport in the UK, it is not yet clear how the process of suspension or expulsion would work in practice, operate with some authority and independence or draw on significant resources.

In relation to exclusivity and privilege, sports development's inclusive approach to practitioners would be challenged if it sought to narrow access to a relatively small group of people due to professional criteria that necessarily have to exclude some and not include all. Furthermore, there are some key questions for consideration for those involved in the development of a sports development profession — if some workers did become recognised as sports development professionals, what would the relationship be between the professionals and volunteers? How would or could someone move from one group to another? And Why would an individual seek to move between groups? Finally, what level of membership of a sports development profession is sustainable and effective in terms of resources, expertise and financial independence?

A response to the CIS Manifesto

In the United Kingdom, trustees from the Institute for Sport, Parks and Leisure (ISPAL) and the ISRM formed a Project Working Group and engaged in a lengthy consultation during 2009–2010, with the aim of establishing a new Chartered Institute of Sport (CIS) in 2011.

> The need for a single institute that is afforded chartered status and that drives professional standards, confidence and credibility within the sector has become increasingly important. (ISRM and ISPAL, 2009: p. 5)

ISRM and ISPAL see the CIS providing advocacy, leadership, raising standards, continuous professional development and career advice, informing government policy, as well as facilitating relationships with both stakeholders and other professions (ISRM and ISPAL, 2009: 5–6). It is anticipated that the CIS will "resolve the lack of clear, coherent and concise representation and recognition for those working in the management, development, strategic planning and administration of sport..." (ISRM and ISPAL, 2009: p. 6). In addition to the benefits mentioned above, the rationale of the CIS makes reference to increased gravitas and profile, one awarding body for professional qualifications, informing government policy and a focus on empirical evidence and research (ISRM and ISPAL, 2009: p. 6). The Comprehensive Spending Review (CSR) undertaken by the UK Coalition Government in Autumn 2010 has made some drastic cuts to public sector spending. This includes funding for sports bodies and a "bonfire of the quangos" (*The Independent* October, 2010: 4–7), and perhaps highlights the necessity of establishing one clear voice in sport that can engage with both government and stakeholders.

The membership of IMSPA appears to be wide-ranging. The CIS will embrace sport and active recreation, indoor and outdoor facilities, as well as major events and tourism (although in another section of the manifesto it refers to sport tourism). In the area of representation the manifesto refers to the importance of ensuring that:

> these professionals — its membership — are correctly represented and positioned at the centre of policy and decision-making to ensure that the fields of sports management and development have the influence and gravitas they warrant. (ISRM and ISPAL, 2009: p. 8)

On the other hand the manifesto is sensitive to the issue of inclusion and the nature of sport, active recreation as a wide-ranging field of disparate groups:

> To represent in accordance with its principle of inclusion, the CIS will be open to all professionals working in the management, administration and development and strategic planning of sport and those who aspire to work in these sectors. (ISRM and ISPAL, 2009: p. 9)

Two levels of membership are proposed. CIS Membership will be open to "anyone working in these areas or indeed those who have aspirations to work in these areas" (ISRM and ISPAL, 2009: p. 11). In contrast, Chartered Membership of the CIS will be "based on a relevant qualification at first degree level" but can also be achieved by "demonstration of significant in-service experience and expertise in areas of the new Institute's remit" (ISRM and ISPAL, 2009: p. 11). Compared to established professions such as medicine or law, this qualification requirement for Chartered Membership seems relatively light. The manifesto sees these "chartered professionals" as leaders of a "vibrant UK-wide sports sector, providing advocacy and leadership and working in partnership with its stakeholders" (ISRM and ISPAL, 2009: p.

7). Who are the 'professionals' or aspiring professionals from sports development expected to apply for Chartered Membership?

One of the guiding principles — excellence — will "govern and inform the design, delivery and enforcement of the educational and qualification opportunities it will offer to its members and the standards by which they operate in industry" (ISRM and ISPAL, 2009: p. 8). Whilst many sport associations focus on certification of leadership and national occupational standards in recent years, ISPAL has taken a further step towards one of the criteria of a profession, that is, the recognition or endorsement of university degrees in the area of sports development at undergraduate level. This is laying important foundations for the new CIS. There is however, little mentioned or clarified, in the 2009 Manifesto, around the expectations for CPD or the criteria for and oversight of suspension or expulsion from the CIS, by a relatively independent Council (equivalent to the General Medical Council), particularly in the category of Chartered Membership.

Throughout the 2009 manifesto there is a range of activities and groups included in the proposed Chartered Institute of Sport. These include sport, physical activity, active recreation, management, development, strategic planning and administration of sport, chartered professionals, volunteers, facilities operations, major events, tourism, and those who aspire to work in the sector. Is this too broad? How will the CIS face the challenge of negotiating with other associations involving practitioners from, for example, events management and tourism? The aim is to have "20,000 members by 2020", ultimately including "25% of those professionals working in the sector", and to be financially sound and sustainable, avoiding financial dependence on government funding (ISRM and ISPAL, 2009: pp. 11–12). Significant progress has been made in joining together ISPAL and ISRM and in securing the commitment of both of these institutes to both the vision and funding of the new CIS. There may be some challenging tensions between recognising social inclusion at the heart of sport and sports development, setting standards and regulatory systems necessary for chartered status, and having a professional body which is self-sufficient and sustainable.

The ISPAL National Occupational Standards (NOS) make a contribution to defining the field of sports development. Though this only goes part way to meeting the rational criteria for a profession laid out by Barker (2010) and Hargreaves (2000) who are concerned not only about agreement on the practical competences and knowledge base for a profession, but also how status, trust and power to include and exclude are established. The NOSs raise interesting questions as the process attempts to gain consensus on what sports development is and therefore what a sports development worker should necessarily know and be able to do at different levels. The question remains about how this will contribute to establishing a profession especially as there is no real pressure or incentive to attain these awards? Would a failure to acquire or update NOSs mean suspension or expulsion, as in established professions?

The CIS's recognition of the real political struggle necessary for the positioning of a body as a profession is likely to culminate in its defining roles that only experts in its field can practice. This would be due to its controls, its standing in the professional community, the specialist knowledge and commitment to care, and ethical conduct that will lead to busy sports spaces, inhabited by a plethora of interested professionals and volunteers needing to consult those experts falling under the auspices of the CIS; that is if the CIS can establish this end game. For sports development, this ability to establish professional governance processes is likely to raise its profile and the status of its 'profession'. It will also enhance gravitas, terms and conditions, due to the supply and demand of expertise, as rewards are restricted to certificated, recognised professionals in a profession.

Sports development must either be part of this process with the CIS or be autonomous in engaging in a similar process unilaterally. At the time of writing the formation of the Institute for the Management of Sport and Physical Activity (IMSPA) was announced and became operational on 1 April, 2011. Membership of ISPAL and ISRM was automatically transferred to the new Institute (IMSPA letter to members at http://www.imspa.co.uk 31 March 2011:1).

The new Institute for the Management of Sport and Physical Activity will have officially opened its doors for business on 1 April, 2011. These are ground-breaking times for the sector as we move towards a more collaborative approach to the representation, support and empowerment of professional working throughout the sport and physical activity sectors. As of this writing in mid 2011, IMSPA is awaiting the decision regarding accreditation by Royal Charter and is already posting details of the continuation of the Continual Professional Development (CPD) Scheme and IMSPA qualifications (see http://www.imspa.co.uk/education). It is interesting that 'coaching' is mentioned in the introduction to the CPD scheme, yet the relationship with or inclusion of 'sport coaching' in the IMSPA was not articulated in the Chartered Institute of Sport manifesto, the IMSPA web site or on the Sports Coach UK web site. There appear to be exciting and challenging times ahead for the IMSPA, dealing with the transitional process, revisiting the original CIS manifesto against the backdrop of the Coalition government, spending reviews, and a range of mergers or restructuring processes in the public sector.

Conclusion

This chapter emerges from ongoing debates concerning career progression, point of entrance, and the place of sports development as a 'profession'. The context and background of sports development together with an overview of its place in Higher Education are also part of the backdrop to this chapter. Although notions of a profession may be viewed differently by various academic disciplines and a range of stakeholders, there is a fair degree of agreement in the literature about what constitutes a profession. These include exclusivity or monopoly of a legally recognised service, developed through a recognised education, where undergraduate and post-graduate courses are followed by recognised and monitored CPD provision. A professional body has the authority to suspend or exclude members who do not meet the standards of competence and ethical conduct required by the profession. It usually involves providing a socially valuable, public service, by people who have a certain set of values and culture, including an altruistic attitude towards providing a public good.

There has been significant and impressive collaboration between ISPAL and ISRM in the development of a manifesto for a Chartered Institute of Sport in the UK, which seeks to outline the benefits, membership categories, structural arrangements, and financing of a Institute for the Management of Sport and Physical Activity. These proposals pay much attention to aims, benefits, engagement with stakeholders and public sport bodies. Progress has already been made by ISPAL on the endorsement or recognition of university degrees in sports development, and this will hopefully continue in the new IMSPA. This is an important feature of a profession. The areas of the manifesto that might benefit from further discussion and development include career progression and associated specialities and salaries, post-graduate education and CPD, systems, roles and authority to suspend and expel, and the relationship and movement between the members and the Chartered Members.

It could be argued that sports development is moving towards the status of a profession, however it is not a profession at this time. At this moment sports development is not a profession beyond one of identity, due to its lack of definition of the field, its lack of a unifying body, no enforceable formal entry criteria, no formal ethical code, and no powers of exclusion or restrictions to practice. In many ways it might better be described as a field of professionals tasked with developing sport in cognate areas. If sports development intends to work toward professional recognition there are significant points here to consider.

Notes

1   The CIS has received privy council approval and gains royal assent on the 11th June 2011.
2   Conducted for Sporting Equals and the Sports Councils.
3   IMPSA is likely to change its name to the Chartered Institute for Managing Sport and Physical Activity after Royal Assent is awarded to the CIS.

References

Australian Council for the Professions (2004) *About Professions Australia: Definition of a profession.* http: //www.professions.com.au/defineprofession.html [accessed 24 November, 2010].

Barber, B. (1965) 'Some problems in the sociology of the professions', in K. Lynn (ed) *The professions in America.* Boston: Baedulus, pp. 669–688.

Barker. R (2010) 'No, management is not a profession', *Harvard Business Review* (July/August): pp. 52–60.

Becher, T. (1999) *Professional practices: Commitment and capability in a changing environment.* New Brunswick, N.J./ London: Transaction.

Broadbent J., Dietrich, M. and Roberts, J. (1997) *The end of the professions?: The restructuring of professional work.* London: Routledge.

Brock, D., and Powell, M., Hinings, C. (eds) (1999) *Restructuring the professional organisation: Accounting, health care and law.* London: Routledge.

Burbules, N. and Densmore, K. (1991) 'The limits of making teaching a profession', *Educational Policy* Vol. 5, No. 1: pp. 44–63.

Collins, M. with Kay, T. (2003) *Sport and social exclusion.* London and New York: Routledge.

CIS (2009) *Chartered Institute of Sport progress update.* London: Institute of Sport and Recreation Management, Institute of Parks, Amenities and Leisure.

Cruess, S., Johnston, S. and Cruess, R. (2004) 'Profession: A working definition for medical educators', *Teaching and Learning in Medicine* Vol. 16, No. 1: pp. 74–76.

Duffy, P. (2009) 'A vision for global coach development: The European and UK examples'. Paper presented to The Global Conference of the International Council for Coach Education, Vancouver.

Duffy, P. Hartley H.J., Bales J. and Crespo M. (2010) 'The development of sports coaching as a profession: Challenges and future directions in a global context', Keynote paper, Petro-Canada Sport Leadership Sportif, Ottawa, Canada, 18 November.

Durkheim, E. (1957) *Professional ethics and civil morals.* London: Routledge and Kegan Paul.

Edwards, L. (2006) 'Power and diversity in public relations', proceedings in Bledcom, *Communicating Europe,* 7–9 July.

Girginov, V. (Ed.) (2008) *Management of sports development.* Oxford: Butterworth-Heinemann.

Hartley, H. J. and Robinson S. J. (2006) Everest ethics; Developing an ethical lens — five ethical theories. Unpublished paper, Leeds Metropolitan University, Leeds, UK.

Hargreaves, A. (2000) 'Four ages of professionalism and professional learning', *Teachers and Teaching: History and Practice* Vol. 6, No. 2: pp. 151–182.

Hawkins, P. (2008) 'The coaching profession: Some of the key challenges', *Coaching: An International Journal of Theory, Research and Practice* Vol. 1, No. 1: pp. 28–38.

Houlihan, B. and Green, M. (eds) (2010) *The Routledge handbook on sports development.* London: Routledge.

Houlihan, B. and White, A. (2002) *The politics of sport development: Development of sport or through sport?* London and New York: Routledge.

Hylton, K. and Bramham, P. (eds) (2008) *Sports development: Policy, process and practice.* London, Routledge.

Hylton, K., Bramham, P., Jackson, D. and Nesti, M. (eds) (2001) *Sports development: Policy, process and practice.* London, Routledge.

Independent (2010) 'Bonfire of the quangos', 15 October: pp. 4–7.

ISRM and ISPAL (2009) *Towards a united and chartered institute of sport: A manifesto for the chartered institute of sport.* London: Institute of Sport and Recreation Management, Institute of Parks, Amenities and Leisure.

Khurana, R. (2010) 'Why management must be a profession', a response to Barker, R. 'No, management is not a profession', 11.10am blog Tuesday 20 July 2010, *Harvard Business Review* at http: // blogs.hbr.org/hbsfaculty/2010/07why-management-must-be-a-profe.html accessed 24/11/2010.

Kennedy, H. (1992) *Eve was framed: Women and British justice.* London: Chatto and Windus.

Krejsler, J. (2005) 'Professions and identities: How to explore professional development among [semi-]professions', *Scandinavian Journal of Educational Research* Vol. 49, No. 4: pp. 335–357.

Larson, M. (1997) *The rise of professionalism: A sociological analysis.* New York: Harper and Row.

Lindop, N. (1982) 'Educational studies and professional authority', *British Journal of Educational Studies* Vol. 30, No. 2: pp. 157–160.

Long, J., Hylton, K., Ratna, A., Spracklen, K, and Bailey, S. (2009) *A systematic review of the literature on black and minority ethnic communities in sport and physical recreation.* Birmingham: Sporting Equals.

Mills, R. (1994) 'The professionalisation of Australian sport: Practice and discussion', *Leisure Options* Vol. 4, No. 2, pp. 43–48.

Patton, M. (1994) 'Professionalism', *Journal of Systems Management*, December: pp. 1–23.

Perkin, H. (1985) 'The teaching profession and the game of life', in P. Gordon (ed) *Is teaching a profession?*. University of London Institute of Education, pp. 12–25.

Pickard, S. (2009) 'The professionalisation of general practitioners with a special interest: Rationalisation, restratification and governmentality', *Sociology* Vol. 43, No. 2: pp. 250–267.

Reed, M. and Anthony, P. (1992) 'Professionalising management and managing professionalisation: British management in the 1980s', *Journal of Management* Vol. 29, No. 9: pp. 591–611.

Rigg, M. (1986) *Action Sport — an evaluation*. London: Sports Council.

Rostrok, S.S. (2009) 'Global initiatives in the coaching field', *An International Journal of Theory, Research and Practice* Vol. 2, No. 1: pp. 76–85.

Smith, C.T. and Westerbeek H.M. (2004) 'Professional sport management education and practice in Australia', *Journal of Hospitality, Leisure, Sport and Tourism* Practice Paper, Vol. 3, No. 2: pp. 38–45.

Sockett, H. (1985) 'Towards a professional code in teaching', in P. Gordon (ed) *Is teaching a profession?*. University of London Institute, pp. 26–43.

Sommerlad, H. (2003) 'Women solicitors in a fractured profession: Intersections of gender and professionalism in England and Wales', *International Journal of the Legal Profession* Vol. 10, No. 1: pp. 213–234.

———— (2009) 'Discourses of diversity, merit and exclusionary practices: Barriers to entry and progression', in L. Cooper and S. Walters (eds) *Critical perspectives, lifelong learning and work*. London: Human Sciences Research Council, pp. 106–122.

Soucie, D. (1994) 'The emergence of sport management as a professional occupation: A North American perspective', *European Journal of Sport Management* Vol. 2, No. 4: pp. 13–30.

Sport England (2002) *Active communities projects: A review of impact and good practice, Edited Summary Report, July 2002*. London: Sport England.

Tobin, N. (2004) 'Can the professionalisation of the UK public relations industry make it more trustworthy?', *Journal of Communication Management* Vol. 9, No. 1: pp. 56–64.

UCAS (2011) Sports Development Courses in the UK, http: //search. ucas.com [Accessed 11th April 2011]

Vollmer, H. and Mills, D. (eds) (1966) *Professionalisation*. New Jersey: Prentice-Hall.

Warrior, R. (2002) 'Reflections of an educational professional', Practice Paper, *Journal of Hospitality, Leisure and Tourism* Vol. 1, No. 2: pp. 57–62.

Wilensky, H.L. (1964) 'The professionalisation of everyone', *American Journal of Sociology* Vol. 70, No. 2: pp. 137–158.

Williams, J. (1998) 'What makes a profession a profession?', *Professional Society* Vol. 43, No. 1: pp. 18–21.

THE INCREASING POLITICISATION OF PHYSICAL EDUCATION AND YOUTH SPORT POLICY: A CASE STUDY OF SCHOOL-CLUB LINKS

Dr Lesley Phillpots* and Dr Jonathan Grix**

*School of Education, University of Birmingham, UK
**Department of Political Science and International Studies,
University of Birmingham, UK

Introduction

Since the 1980s, the school and youth sport policy area has been transformed from a relatively neglected backwater to a burgeoning and increasingly complex and politicised arena. The Labour Government's strategy for sport *A Sporting Future for All* (April 2000) proved to be the catalyst for a number of national initiatives that were intended to change the way in which physical education and youth sport were resourced. In a joint press release by the DfES and the DCMS on the 11th January 2001, the Government outlined its commitment to 'giving children a sporting chance' by offering them access both during and after school to high quality coaching and the opportunity to take part in competitive sports within and between schools. In addressing these policy objectives the Government set out its plan to raise standards of physical education and school sport. This was instigated through a five point plan that focused on rebuilding new school sport facilitates, the creation of 110 Specialist Sports Colleges, extension of sporting opportunities beyond the school day (through an allocation of £240 million), the establishment of 600 school sport co-ordinators linked wherever possible to a Specialist Sports College, and access for talented 14–18 year olds to coaching and support (DfES, 2001). The Labour Government also increased the availability of funding for school sport and physical education through extending the New Deal initiative (a key part of the Government's Welfare to Work Strategy) into schools. A commitment was also made to the creation of two thousand opportunities for suitable people from New Deal to work in schools alongside School Sports Co-ordinators by the year 2004. In addition, the New Deal for Schools initiative also provided £1.1 billion for capital works projects that targeted improvements to school sports facilities. These plans signified a renewed investment in, and change to, the resourcing of physical education and heralded fundamental changes in the way school and youth sport was staffed, delivered and resourced (DfES, 2003; Houlihan and Green, 2006).

A fundamental objective of Specialist Sports Colleges was to raise standards of teaching and learning in school sport and physical education. The specialist schools concept was built upon a model of partnership and a family of schools working together in order to secure whole school improvement. Sports Colleges were required to help and provide benefits to other schools in their local area, to provide sports resources for the wider community, to strengthen their links between private and/or charitable sponsors and to extend the range of opportunities available to children. Houlihan (2000) has highlighted the inherent difficulties and challenges faced by Specialist Sports Colleges in their position at the intersection of multiple policy agendas and interests. Their responsibilities included raising standards in schools, educationalists' concerns with the learning needs and achievements of all children, the concerns of NGBs for sport development and the identification and development of sporting talent. Agencies and organisations, such as the Youth Sport Trust, the DCMS, the DfES, the New Opportunities Fund and Sport England were just some of the bodies that were actively involved in ensuring the delivery of the Government's objectives in association with Specialist Sports Colleges.

The School Sport Co-ordinator programme was established as an initiative that reflected the Government's desire to achieve joined-up policy-making between government departments. In June 1999, the Government announced a multi-agency initiative in which six hundred new Schools Sport Co-ordinators were to be appointed to help arrange competitive fixtures between schools and to help boost after-school sports. Speaking at the Institute for Public Policy Research Conference in 1999 on its *Vision for Sport in the UK*, Schools Minister Charles Clarke said that it would be the job of the School Sports Co-ordinator to lift the pressure on teachers by arranging better links between schools and sports clubs to increase after school sport. The programme was established as a joint collaboration between Sport England, DCMS, DfEE (now the DfE), the New Opportunities Fund and the Youth Sport Trust (YST). Its key objectives involved strategic planning, primary liaison, school and community, coaching and leadership and raising standards. The preferred model of delivery for the programme was through a family of schools built around a cluster of secondary, primary and special schools. In this model, a typical partnership might consist of one Partnership Development Manager (PDM), four School Sport Co-ordinators and twenty Primary Link Tutors. A PDM was identified within the Sports College or LEA to support and manage the development of local partnership arrangements. The scale of financial investment in the School Sport Co-ordinator programme signalled the Government's intention that it should play a key role in developing the Government's strategy for physical education and sport for young people and consolidated the linkages between a variety of sporting agencies, sports bodies and schools.

The launch of the national Physical Education, School Sport and Club Links (PESSCL) strategy in 2002 through a joint DfES and DCMS Public Service Agreement (PSA) target represented a major commitment by the Labour Government to school sport. Later re-named the Physical Education and Sport Strategy for Young People (PESSYP) strategy, it was a youth sport infrastructure for England delivered at local level through collaborative arrangements between a range of PE and sport agencies. The initiative was funded by the Department for Education (DfE) and the Department for Culture, Media and Sport (DCMS) and jointly managed on their behalf by the Youth Sport Trust (YST) and Sport England (SE). The overall aim of the programme was to help local partners to increase the provision, demand and take-up of sport amongst all young people in England. Later the strategy also focused on an Olympic legacy aim to get more young people taking part in high quality physical education and sport through an offer of five hours a week of high-quality PE and sport for 5–16 year olds. The PESSYP strategy included ten key work strands, each designed to maximise opportunities for young people to access high-quality PE and sport and, in accordance with other policy areas, its outcomes were managed through Government imposed Public Service Agreement (PSA) targets delivered locally through partnership arrangements between schools, local authorities, national governing bodies of sport, sport clubs and sport development agencies. The question remained however as to how these new funding arrangements between Government, education and sport agencies would shape the delivery and policy outcomes of the initiative (MacDonald, 2002).

A growing body of political scientists argue that 'new' governance arrangements for public policy delivery and implementation have brought about the erosion of central governmental power and with it, the state's ability to determine and deliver policy (Bevir and Rhodes,

2006; 2008; Skelcher, 2000). However despite this rhetoric of a shift from strong, unitary Government to governance by and through networks and partnerships, it obscures the reality of governance arrangements which have close ties to, and regulation from, the centre (Bevir and Rhodes, 2003, 2006, 2008). Whilst PE and youth sport delivery and implementation is ostensibly conducted through a variety of arms' length para-statal bodies such as Sport England and the Youth Sport Trust, their involvement appears tightly managed and centrally controlled by Government. As we have argued elsewhere, the PE and youth sport policy area is weak and is characteristic of a sector that is a 'policy taker' and not a 'policy maker' (see Goodwin and Grix, 2011; Grix and Phillpots, 2011). Indeed, Houlihan (2000) describes PE and youth sport in England is a highly complex and politicised policy area that is subject to pressure from a range of competing sectoral interests.

In order to examine the governance arrangements for PE and youth sport, the empirical element of our study includes two micro-case studies of athletics and golf. They represent two NGBs that have been involved in the School Club Links (SCL) work strand of the PESSYP strategy from its early stages. The case studies provide empirical insight into the governance and structural arrangements of a complex range of agencies involved in policy delivery. The intention is to assess the extent to which policy actors such as schools and NGBs have had the capacity to exercise control over School Club Links policy implementation. Finally, we examine the extent to which the SCLs work strand has become a policy area that represents what Clarke and Stewart (1999) and Stoker (1999) suggest is indicative of locally determined 'community governance' through local agencies, or an arena that is subject to increasing centralised government intervention and control.

In order to contextualise the policy context for PE and youth sport, a brief historical account of the political continuities, changes and public sector policy priorities for youth sport and physical education leading up to the formation of the School Club Links work strand is provided.

The policy background to the School Club Links work strand

The seminal Report of the Wolfenden Committee on Sport (1960) highlighted the inadequacy in the provision of youth sport outside curriculum time and, in particular, drew attention to weaknesses in the links between PE in schools and sports clubs. This problem, commonly known as 'the gap', was used to exemplify the marked break between the norms of participation in physical activity of young people inside schools and the lack of comparable sporting activities available in community contexts. The failure of a range of policy actors and agencies to resolve this 'gap' and achieve systematic linkages within youth sport provision was indicative of intransigent jurisdictional disputes between successive governments, schools and sports clubs.

Henry (1993) and Houlihan (1997) argue that there was a marked change in the British Government's approach to sport post 1991. An important factor was John Major's personal interest in sport and the belief that sport and school sport could make a contribution to the achievement of the Conservative Government's broader political agenda. John Major's administration was keen to create a more coherent and dynamic approach to policy for sport and the arts. Conservative Government and media concern about the parlous state of sporting opportunities and the increasing loss of school playing fields during the mid 1990s gave rise to public concerns about an apparent crisis in youth sport (Roberts, 1995). The publication of *Sport: Raising the Game* in 1995 established youth sport and sporting excellence as two government priorities. In the preface to the document, John Major acknowledged that the publication of this sports policy statement represented the most significant set of government proposals ever produced for sport (DNH, 1995). Significantly, it placed a "twin emphasis on school sport and excellence" (Houlihan, 2000: p. 174) and laid the foundations for many new sporting developments and partnerships in which schools played a crucial role in achieving the Conservative Government's agenda for sport. The establishment of a National Lottery through the National Lottery Act (1993) enabled the Government to provide additional funding for sport and heralded a clear shift in government policy (Houlihan, 2000). The publication of *Sport: Raising the Game* provided an organisational, financial and administrative framework that was intended to shape the future direction of sport policy in the twenty-first century (Green, 2004).

In 1996, the Sports Council launched the National Junior Sports programme aimed at young people between the ages of 5 and 18. The programme was organised through schools and the local community with support from organisations including the Youth Sports Trust and the National Coaching Foundation. The creation in 1994 of the Youth Sport Trust as a registered charity to create opportunities for all young people to receive a quality introduction to physical education and sport through activity based programmes was to have a major effect on arrangements for youth sport policy. The Trust, through its substantial financial backing from Sir John Beckwith and the dynamic leadership of its CEO Sue Campbell, was in a unique financial position to develop school sport, at a time when resources and finances in schools were limited. A key feature of the YST's work with schools were its TOPS programme that provided free in-service training for primary school teachers, resource cards and sports equipment. Whilst relatively simple concepts, the development of the TOP PLAY and TOP SPORT programmes from 1995 onwards made a significant impact in schools and created the need for an infrastructure to support it. These programmes and other initiatives such as Champion Coaching (a youth sport coaching programme run by the National Coaching Foundation) had been effective in bringing together a number of key sporting agencies, such as sports clubs, coaches, schools and national governing bodies, to work in partnership to improve youth participation in sport. They helped to create an early platform for the development of a national strategy for school sport. This, coupled with the activities that brought Sue Campbell into contact with government departments, led to what was to be a fortuitous decision by the YST to take on the management of specialist sports colleges. With its growing access to DfES and the success of its work with the first group of sports colleges, the YST had obtained a growing reputation of successful delivery. In the absence of any other obvious competitor, the Trust found itself in a unique position in which it was able to harness the support of senior ministers and also gain support from Number 10 for the potential difference that sport could make to the lives of young people. The capacity to deliver both education and sport outcomes through youth sport was crucial in helping the YST to secure funding from DfES for the Physical Education, School Sport and Club Links strategy (PESSCL) (Phillpots, 2007, unpublished. PhD thesis).

The period from the mid 1980s onwards was characterised by increasing political interest in PE and youth sport and the publication of a range of official government sport policy documents (see **Table 1** for an overview of historical developments). The most significant political contribution to a more structured and cohesive framework for the development of PE and youth sport in England was undoubtedly the creation of a formal strategy for physical education and school sport.

The Physical Education, School Sport and Club Links (PESSCL) strategy

The launch of the national Physical Education, School Sport and Club Links (PESSCL) strategy in 2002 represented a major commitment by

Table 1   *Overview of historical developments*

Year	Document/ seminar	Written/ commis- sioned by	Main theme
1966–1984	'Sport for All'	Sports Council	The problem of school to club links was exacerbated by a sport policy context in the late 1980s and early 1990s in which schools, the sports lobby, the Sports Council and the Central Council for Physical Recreation (CCPR) operated as independent agencies with no coherent vision for youth sport.
1986	'Sports in Schools' *Desk Study*	DoES, Sports Council	Clubs lacked structures, capacity and willingness to develop closer club-school links
1995	'Sport: Raising the Game'	Department of National Heritage	Sets out Sport Council's new responsibility for promoting school to club links by providing advice, support and information to schools, the national governing bodies of sport, sports clubs and local authorities. Need for NGBs to include school sport projects as a condition of Sports Council funding (DNH, 1995:8).
1995	'PE and Sport: A Survey of Good Practice'	Ofsted	Highlighted that links between schools and local sport clubs were sometimes strong, sometimes tenuous and occasionally non-existent and, whilst some schools had forged links with clubs overall the process was deemed ad hoc.
2000	'A Sporting Future For All'	DCMS	Created a policy context in which both sport and educational bodies were actively encouraged to work in partnership to achieve shared objectives. Sports clubs were targeted for reform and the strategy document highlighted the 'need for a much more professional club structure to complement the role of schools' (DCMS, 2000: 13). **Impact on club-Schools link:** Brought about change and a more professional approach to the management of clubs.
2002	'Game Plan'	DCMS	Highlighted the Government's willingness to intervene in the case of failures in the delivery of sport and where there were 'inefficiencies and inequities which provided a rationale for government intervention in sport' (DCMS/ Strategy Unit, 2002: 76). **Impact on club-Schools link:** Represents a turning point in Government intervention in sport; a more co-ordinated, national approach to planning for sport. It was to be achieved through a new, contractual, national governing body, delivery framework.

the Labour Government to restructuring the delivery of youth sport in England (Flintoff, 2003). Its overall objective was framed by a joint DfES and DCMS Public Service Agreement (PSA) target:

> ...to enhance the take up of sporting opportunities by 5–16 year olds. The aim is to increase the percentage of school children in England who spend a minimum of two hours each week on high quality PE and school sport within and beyond the curriculum to 75 per cent by 2006. (DfES, 2003: p. 2)

The over-arching strategy was administered through a board of representatives comprised of professional PE associations, head teachers, the Office for Standards in Education (OFSTED), the Qualifications and Curriculum Authority (QCA), Sport England, DCMS, DfES and NGBs. The strategy initially included nine inter-linked work strands: Sports Colleges, School Sport Partnerships, School/Club Links, the Gifted and Talented Programme, the QCA PE and School Sport Investigation, Step into Sport, Swimming, Sporting Playgrounds and Professional Development. Funded predominantly by the Treasury, the Labour Government initially committed £459 million to the PESSCL strategy, with an additional allocation of £686 million to improve school sport facilities across England (DfES/ DCMS, 2003). Monitored by the Prime Minister's Delivery Unit (PMDU) in its first 18 months of operation, the PESSCL strategy reported to the Prime Minister's Delivery Unit (PMDU), rather than to the Treasury; a requirement that reflected its status as a key political policy priority.

The management and implementation of the School-Club Links Work Strand

The School Club Links work strand was a constituent part of the PESSCL strategy and was framed by a joint DfES and DCMS Public Service Agreement (DCMS/DfES, 2002) whose target was to increase the percentage of 5 to 16 year olds who were members of national governing body accredited sports clubs from 14% in 2002, to a target of 25% by 2008. Twenty-two NGBs initially received funding from Sport England to help clubs develop sustainable and effective links with schools. School Club links arrangements were formalised through contractual relationships and Public Service Agreements (PSAs) between NGBs, sports clubs and schools. The funding mechanisms, patterns of accountability and delivery of the work strand reflected the Labour Government's overriding political desire for efficiency, transparency and accountability in public sector services.

Delivery of the School Club Links work strand was through partnership arrangements between NGBs and sports clubs with SSPs providing the structural framework for the delivery of the School Club Links work strand. It was jointly managed by Sport England and the Youth Sport Trust on behalf of DCMS. Sport England monitored the implementation of the initiative through a mechanism whereby NGBs reported their progress in achieving Government imposed targets on a monthly basis.

Methodology

The National Governing Body Case Studies

The selection of two NGBs and their involvement with the SCLs work strand provides the empirical context for our examination of the politicisation of PE and youth sport policy. Athletics and golf represented Sport England Priority Sports[1] and were the recipients of significant government funding that was linked to the delivery of the outcomes of the School Club Links work strand. Important policy developments in each case are examined and the negotiations, tensions, resistance and policy shifts that have occurred in these sports in the time period framed by the SCLs work strand are outlined.

We adopt an epistemological approach termed 'hard' interpretivism: that is, we see our work on the border of critical realist and interpretivist epistemology (for further explanation of this see Grix, 2010; Goodwin and Grix, 2011). This has ramifications for what we seek to uncover in this paper and how we go about it (see Marsh and Furlong, 2002, 18). We are not attempting to produce a 'representative' or statistically significant study from two NGBs; rather, we offer some insights from two NGBs into the wider process of the politicisation of sport. We value the experiences, values and attitudes of key actors working closely with School-Club links (see Burnham *et. al.*, 2008, 246–7). Effectively, then, we are taking a small snap-shot of a much wider process: the politicisation of sport. School Club Links is, of course, not unique in being politicised. In recent work we have unpicked the political development of County Sport Partnerships and how sport policy has been directed from the Treasury down to street-level bureaucrats (see Grix and Phillpots, 2011). On the other hand, elite (Olympic) sport is probably the most politicised, with governments investing heavily into this in an attempt to gain international prestige and the elusive 'feelgood factor' (see Grix and Carmichael, 2011).

Part of the empirical data presented in this micro-study is drawn from nine in-depth interviews from 2005–2010 with policy actors from a range of government, sport and education agencies that had been involved in the PESSYP strategy and the School Club Links work strand for at least five years. Please note this does not include inter-viewees 3, 6 and 7 below. Interviewee 3 had 2 year's experience with School Club Links; interviewees 6 and 7 were only indirectly involved in the policy, but were able to comment on its outcome. All other interviewees were selected on the basis of their direct involvement in this policy area. They are listed in **Table 2** along with their positions, organisations, gender and interview type.

We employed in-depth, semi-structured and (mostly) taped (with the exception of 3) interviews, using a similar interview schedule. The choice of semi-structured interviews, however, allowed us to remain flexible in the order of questions asked and to be able to pose additional, actor-specific questions when they arose. We suggest that the interview technique is a useful addition to a study. However, if possible, this method ought not be the sole source of data, but should be supplemented by other research methods and data. This we do by contextualising the interviews in a systematic and chronological analysis of a range of government policy documents, NGB annual reports and inspection evidence from quangos such as Sport England and the Youth Sport Trust (YST). Our approach to these texts is a simple one: we have read and found trends of the politicisation of

Table 2   Interviewees' experience

Interviewee	Institution/ Agency	Male/ Female	Type of Interview
1 CEO	Professional Golf Association	Male	In-depth, taped
2 School-club-links manager	Professional Golf Association	Male	In-depth, taped
3 Head, school-club links	England Athletics	Male	In-depth, not taped
4 Senior employee	Professional Golf Association	Male	In-depth, taped
5 School Club Links Project Manager	UK Athletics	Female	In-depth, taped
6 (Former) International Distance Runner	n/a	Male	Email response to interview schedule
7 Senior athletics coach	UK Athletics	Male	In-depth, taped
8 Athletics statistician	Umbro Limited	Male	In-depth, not taped
9 Senior Civil Servant	Civil Service	Male	In-depth, taped

sport policy. The SCL work strand was selected as a case study as it involves sport and education agencies in complex fiscal arrangements and the delivery of shared government imposed policy outcomes. Athletics was selected because of its long tradition as part of the curriculum of schools; in comparison the game of golf had limited links with schools and had lobbied hard to be included in the SCLs work strand.

Athletics

Background and context

For athletics, the timing of the launch of the PESSCL strategy in 2002 coincided with a modernisation project as a consequence of the recommendations of the Foster Report, *Moving On* (2004), commissioned by UK Sport and Sport England. The report suggested that the sport's structural arrangements required wholesale modernisation and also highlighted the failure of athletics to stem the continued decline in participation rates amongst young people. The report also revealed disagreement within the governing body regarding the purpose of athletics and whether its role was to service the demands of elite sport or mass participation (Foster Report, 2004). Whilst it was acknowledged that athletics was a key element in the Government's plans to expand school sport, there were concerns expressed within the report about the declining health and status of athletics in schools. The report highlighted systemic problems, as "within athletics clubs there is an issue about their configuration: with schools the issue is about what they do" (Foster Report, 2004: p. 27). The failure of athletics clubs to understand and fully engage with school sport was compounded by strong perceptions that traditional school sports such as athletics were beginning to lose their popularity amongst young people (Roberts, 1996). Indeed a recent study into the reasons behind the decline in athletics performances at elite level (Grix and Parker, 2010) highlighted the declining role that school sport played in nurturing talent and creating potential champions. One interviewee, a leading senior athletics coach, suggested that "30 years ago I believe 95% of children who had running talent got a taste of the sport [athletics] via school sports, school teams, District/County schools champs [championships] or attendance at some sort of local [running] club. I would estimate that the percentage nowadays is less than 20%" (Interview, March, 2008). An ex-international distance runner offered a reason for the decline in popularity of athletics: a plethora of "Soccer Schools of Excellence are a plague eating away at potential talent recruitment and development in other sports in the UK" (Interview, April, 2008).

School-club links

Set against a background of internal upheavals within UK Athletics and a process of modernisation, the Athletics School to Club Links Programme was rolled out across England in April 2004. Although the sport was initially reluctant to become part of the SCL programme due to internal management issues, athletics was eventually one of the first recipients of SCL funding. The School Club Links Project Director for UK Athletics described how Sport England "selected the Big Four sports first and then athletics, swimming and gymnastics; it was significant that our Assistant CEO also sat on the Coaching Task Force" (Interview: June 2006). Furthermore she explained how in its first year delivering the SCL programme, UK Athletics received £56k to forge 36 links between schools and athletics clubs in 9 of its regions. The investment significantly increased to £400k per annum over the next two years (Interview, June, 2006). The award to UK Athletics was agreed by Sport England and amounted to £415,000, with £315,000 used for NGB staff salaries and £100,000 allocated to CSPs to support the delivery of the programme.

The Labour Government's policy of 'professionalising' sport agencies involved the modernisation of NGB operations through carrot and stick funding mechanisms that also required NGBs to drive reform in sports clubs (Sport England, 2004). The School Club Links Project Director for athletics highlighted the challenges of working with amateur volunteers in their clubs who lacked the time, skills and experience to produce the detailed documentation demanded as a consequence of funding for the work strand. UK Athletics managed its School Club Links programme primarily through CSPs with delivery co-ordinated through English Regional Development Co-ordinators and Partnership Athletics Development Officers (PADOs). One PADO expressed reservations about the overly bureaucratic nature of the club links programme in which:

> Funding doesn't get down to the individual club or school in most cases: it goes on the structures, to support officers and the work of CSPs. There remains a lack of funding for schools and for equipment to deliver the SCLs initiative. (Interview, June 2006)

The structural and personnel changes created as a consequence of the modernisation of UK Athletics' coincided with parallel changes to the infrastructure for PE and School Sport. With its internal review processes and staffing changes in full swing, engaging with the SCL work strand proved to be challenging for athletics.

Recent developments

The announcement in 2005 of the London 2012 Olympics led to a re-focusing of sport policy and subsequent drives to modernise sport agencies so they were fit for purpose (see Houlihan and Green, 2009; Hylton and Bramham, 2007). As a consequence of the completion of the modernisation process in 2008, England Athletics (EA) assumed responsibility for the delivery of grass-roots athletics, with UK Athletics managing the crucial transition of young people from junior to senior level competition. The SCLs work strand represented just one of a number of programmes designed to increase the visibility and popularity of athletics amongst young people. The member of staff in charge of the school club work strand at English Athletics highlighted the challenges faced by all NGBs in a process of "long-term change ... driven by short-term government NGB funding". The central concern for athletics was to ensure the long-term sustainability of the School to Club Links initiative given the short term nature of funding and the lack of targeted funding for SCLs in the new policy arrangements as the PESSCL strategy metamorphosed into the PESSYP strategy (Interview, March, 2010).

Measuring success

The challenge for the SCLs initiative was that policy outcomes take years to come to fruition and given the climate of 'evidence-based' policy in which most publicly funded organisations operate, there is a necessity to deliver policy that 'works' (Sanderson, 2002; see also Smith and Leech, 2010). Whilst statistics are notoriously problematic, they do indicate general trends. Of approximately 110,000 individuals affiliated to English Athletics, the demographics highlight a significant drop in numbers that make the transition to club sport after the age of 16 (source: EA booklet, 2010):

Age	Number of competing athletes
11–16	23, 000
17–24	8, 000
25–34	13, 000
35+	55, 000

Indeed these figures are generally indicative of a common pattern across most sports and are reflected in statistics published in the ongoing Sport England Active People Survey that commenced in 2005. The rate of attrition from athletics after 16 years of age has a significant impact on the depth of talent in athletics, with consequently lowered standards at county, area, national cross-country championships and national track competitions (see Orme, 2005; Gains, 2009).

The Head of School Club Links at England Athletics stated that, amongst the younger cohorts of athletes, affiliated members grew by 4,000 in the period from June 2009 to June 2010 as a result of significant investment in initiatives to improve the transfer of school children to clubs (Interview, March 2010). However, whilst EA achieved its target of 250 club-school link agreements set by Sport England, EA's Head of School Club Links suggested that a better indicator of whether School Club Links have been successful is the standard of individual athletic performances recorded on the UK Athletics sponsored 'Power of 10' website (http: //www.thepowerof 10.info/).

Golf

Background and context

Golf's relationship with schools began in the 1950s as a response to a decline in levels of participation in the game generally and a significant reduction in the membership of golf clubs specifically. Keen to address these problems, the golf correspondent Henry Longhurst suggested that the solution was for golf was to actively work in partnership with schools (Golf Foundation, 2007). The success of a pilot partnership golf scheme with schools convinced Longhurst and members of the Professional Golfers' Association (PGA) that it was possible to make golf instruction available through a process of fund-raising and subsidy. The creation of the Golf Foundation in 1953 and the subsequent publication of its first Progress Report in August of the same year described how "108 Schools and other educational establishments had registered for Golf Foundation instruction, representing around 3500 young people becoming actively involved in the sport of golf" (Golf Foundation, 2007). With the success of the venture and the exponential growth of interest in golf within schools, the demand for instruction quickly outstripped the funding available. In its Progress Report (1953–4) the Golf Foundation outlined its predicament: "At least another 100 schools are eager and waiting to start. But we cannot expand to include them without more contributions to our funds" (Golf Foundation, 2007). Since that time, the work of the Golf Foundation has remained limited by its own capacity to raise funds and by the restrictions imposed upon it by schools and the introduction of a National Curriculum for Physical Education (NCPE) in 1989, which did not include golf within the PE syllabus (Interview, July 2006). As a consequence, the governing bodies responsible for golf in England had to rely on their own financial resources and internal structures to develop young people's interest in golf. It was not until the launch of the well funded PESSCL school sport strategy in 2003 that golf had the opportunity to secure money for the development of youth golf via the School Club Links work strand.

Early stages of school club links

The allocation of considerable Government funding to athletics, cricket, tennis and rugby to deliver the SCLs work strand galvanised members of golf's governing bodies to lobby for its inclusion in the programme. A Senior Member of the Golf Foundation recollected how civil servants directly involved in the PESSCL strategy were invited to 'The Open' in order to discuss golf's inclusion in the Club Links programme. A senior employee who was working in schools for the Golf Foundation at the time, recollected how:

> People heard about [the SCL work strand] by rumour; then the 'Big Four' tennis, cricket, rugby, football announced they had secured significant funding from Government, certainly in the millions, to deliver the Club Link Programme. So golf decided to do some lobbying of its own and we invited the Civil Servant in overall charge of the PESSCL programme to The Open Championship. (Interview: June 2006)

However, when the PESSCL initiative was launched in 2003, civil servants made it clear that the sport was not fit for purpose as there was no unitary body that represented golf. At a meeting between a senior member of the Professional Golfers' Association (PGA) and a Senior Civil Servant working for DCMS, a case was made for golf to become involved in the SCLs programme. The Chief Executive of the Golf Foundation described how it became clear that Government was not prepared to work with, and fund those sports whose governance arrangements were complex and unwieldy. It was clear that politically, if golf wanted to become the recipient of government funding, then it needed to create a single body for golf (Interview: July 2006). Prior to its involvement with the PESSCL strategy, golf had four governing bodies: the English Golf Union (EGU) (the men's amateur body), English Ladies Golf Association (ELGA) (the women's amateur body), the Professional Golfers' Association (PGA) (professional golf) and the Golf Foundation (junior golf). With pressure from Government to modernise and reform, and a desire within the game to seek new opportunities to grow the game, golf established the England Golf Partnership (EGP) in 2005 as an umbrella organisation. The EGP's role was to co-ordinate one development plan for golf in England, more commonly referred to as a 'Whole Sport Plan'. Establishing this partnership organisation meant that golf secured investment from Sport England, the arms length agency through which the Government implemented and financed community sports policy.

The Chief Executive of the Golf Foundation suggested that the creation of one body for golf meant that Sport England was happy to fund the sport as there was now a single vision for the game. Modernisation proved to be the catalyst for England Golf's involvement in a range of government funded initiatives through programmes such as the PESSCL strategy. There was an acknowledgement that golf had been politically naïve in the past and that the formation of a single association was an astute move that strengthened its capacity to deliver golf to young people (Interview: CEO Golf Foundation, July 2006).

School club links

Golf's desire to engage with schools and to grow the game was exemplified in the Golf Foundation's Annual Report (2004) which highlighted the issues and challenges facing the game. The traditional golf club was under threat and experiencing a shortage of members, in part due to a historical legacy whereby clubs had failed to be proactive in encouraging young players and beginners to enter the game. Whilst money was not regarded as the main 'raison d'être' behind golf's engagement with the Club Links initiative, it was acknowledged that Government funding offered golf greater security and the capacity to plan longer term. As the EGU and ELGA only worked in club settings, the Golf Foundation was the obvious choice to lead on the initiative as it was already active as a golf charity working mainly with primary schools. The Golf Foundation's Programme Manager for the SCLs strategy explained the motivation behind golf's desire to get involved in the work strand:

> The main reason for investing in the Club Links programme was that we wanted to increase the participation rate of young people in the sport, in an area (schools) where we traditionally couldn't recruit. What we wanted to do was to recruit from a sector that wouldn't ordinarily play, in order to broaden the participation rate of the age group. (Interview: June 2006)

Partnership Development Managers (PDMs) employed by School Sport Partnerships played a key, strategic role in golf's SCLs programme and were given ownership of the project through the allocation of £2,000 for each partnership of Sport England funding through the EGP which was managed on its behalf by the Golf Foundation. As part of a written agreement between PDMs and the Golf Foundation, both agencies co-ordinated SCLs projects in partnership with accredited golf clubs (Interview: CEO Golf Foundation, July 2006). The approach of the Golf Foundation was to position itself so that it delivered what teachers and schools wanted:

> We are now in receipt of £120,000 for SCL so it's gone from £80,000 to £120,000 in 3 years; we've had a £40,000 increase. We have appointed a PESSCL co-ordinator who helps with the administrative side of processing applications. We allocated £2,000 per partnership, which is not a lot of money, but it acts as a kind of sweetener, pump-priming funding because the schools have bought into golf and see what golf can offer them; they start to use their own money, apply for Big Lottery Fund (BLF) money and start doing it for themselves so it becomes quite sustainable. (Interview: Golf Foundation School Club Links Manager, June 2006)

The funding for the School Links programme was channelled through SSPs and was managed by a Partnership Development Manager who was required by the EGP to provide quarterly updates on their School Club Links grant. As an added incentive for schools and/or PDMs to complete their annual evaluation report, projects returning their monitoring forms were eligible to receive an additional £1,000 grant. Golf's decision to work directly with SSPs and through PDMs was acknowledged as being at odds with Sport England's advice to work through County Sports Partnerships:

Measuring success

The success of golf's SCLs programme attracted comment from senior politicians such as Alan Johnson who, as Secretary of State for Education at the Sports Colleges Conference in February 2007, reported that "while football, cricket and athletics remained the bedrock of school sport, the number of pupils playing golf had increased by 64% in the past three years" (*The Times*, Friday 2nd February 2007). The management and implementation of golf's School Links programme did however have some inherent tensions. As an NGB, golf felt pressurised by Sport England to forge relationships with County Sport Partnerships, which golf regarded as an unnecessary level of bureaucracy through which Sport England wished to direct and monitor delivery of the SCLs initiative.

In its Annual Report (2005) the Golf Foundation suggested that its most significant development since 2004 had been the increase in the amount of golf that took place within schools, particularly primary schools (Golf Foundation, Annual Report, 2004). For an NGB that was heavily reliant upon volunteer staff and a small workforce to promote youth golf, involvement in the SCLs work strand introduced a new culture of bureaucratic monitoring and reporting systems. The Golf Foundation's School Club Links Manager suggested that:

> Whilst I don't have a huge issue with target setting, I do have a problem with the levels of bureaucracy that are involved with Government money and I think a lot of governing bodies spend a huge amount of time on paperwork and bureaucracy. (Interview: June, 2006)

However it should also be acknowledged that whilst the DCMS, through Sport England, kept a close eye on Government contributions to the EGP by seeking assurances that taxpayers' money was being spent in a way they would approve, golf as a sport was also a real beneficiary of this investment. Independent surveys conducted for the Department of Children, Families and Schools (DCFS) revealed that golf was one of the fastest growing sports in schools in the period 2004 to 2008 as participation in that period increased from 14% to 38% (TNS, 2006). Golf had maximised the opportunity offered by the SCLs work strand and from 2006 onwards, school participation in golf rose from 14 to 42%; 10,000 teachers and 3,500 'young leaders' were trained by the Golf Foundation helping to bridge the gap between golf clubs and schools (*The Daily Telegraph*, 14th July, 2010).

Conclusion

Our empirical work provides a useful insight into the policy process and the increasing politicisation of PE and youth sport in England. As our research was underpinned by hard interpretivist assumptions, our attention was directed towards an understanding of policy change that was cognisant both of the structural conditions and the role of agents in shaping policy and its implementation. In acknowledging the antecedent social structures and conditions prior to the launch of the PESSCL strategy in 2002, there was evidence of growing political advocacy for PE and youth sport. However, it was not until the invest-ment of ring-fenced Treasury funding that formal structural links between schools and clubs were established across a range of sports.

The political climate in which the PESSCL strategy emerged, and the availability of funding as a consequence of the establishment of sport as a National Lottery 'good cause' in 1994, undoubtedly allowed Government to support PE and youth sport policies such as the SCLs initiative. Significantly, its launch coincided with a shift in the Labour

Government's approach to public sector delivery which focused explicitly upon policy outcomes and quantifiable performance indicators and target setting (Deem and Brehony, 2005). The PESSCL strategy and the SCLs work strand undoubtedly operated in a political context in which the Labour Government's approach to public service delivery was framed by the White Paper *Modernising Government* (Cabinet Office: 1999). This policy document encouraged greater co-operation and co-ordination across departmental boundaries through joined-up government and a seamless delivery of public services. These systemic changes meant that the Secretaries of State at that time, Charles Clarke (DfES) and Tessa Jowell (DCMS) were accountable and closely involved in target setting and policy delivery within their respective departments. The PESSCL strategy's joint DfES/DCMS PSA (2003) target was indicative of this new approach to policy delivery and represented an innovative and pioneering attempt to bring together two government departments to deliver a new national strategy for physical education and youth sport. Significantly, Sue Campbell's appointment as subject advisor to the Labour Government on PE and sport, which involved working across the two departments (DfES and DCMS), was a ground-breaking piece of policy-making that meant that the YST now had a cross department advisory role to play between education and sport. In May 2003, during his opening speech to the Central Council for Physical Recreation (CCPR), the Minister for Sport Richard Caborn set the parameters for a new sport policy context in which the Labour Government watchwords were delivery, efficiency, transparency and accountability. Government was entering into new partnership arrangements with education and sport agencies which meant that "sport must now prove its worth and demonstrate in a transparent manner what it can achieve ... I am confident sport will continue to rise to this challenge" (Richard Caborn, Opening Speech at CCPR Conference, 20 May 2003).

Our micro case studies highlight how two sport agencies involved in the SCL's work strand operated in a policy context in which Government exercised tight fiscal control over the use of public funds through arm's-length organisations and quangos such as Sport England, CSPs and the YST whose role was to distribute or withhold public funds based upon performance outcomes. The funding of all the agencies involved in delivering the SCLs work strand was tightly managed by Sport England through the use of Whole Sport Plans and Key Performance Indicators. Our study suggests that Sport England used the opportunity afforded by these new structural conditions to exercise greater control over the work of NGBs and schools.

What also emerges from our research is evidence of the increasing use by Sport England of County Sports Partnerships as local delivery agencies over which it exercised tight control (see Grix and Phillpots, 2011). Our data suggest however that CSPs were regarded as an unnecessary layer of bureaucracy through which Sport England attempted to manage and control the work of SSPs and NGBs. These tightly managed governance arrangements were indicative of increasing bureaucratic control of PE and youth sport through intermediary para-statal organisations who were strategically positioned and funded by Government to achieve targets and the delivery of "an active and successful sporting nation" (Sport England, 2006: p. 4). Indeed the introduction of PSA targets and KPIs into the youth sport policy area allowed Sport England in particular to gain more power and control over the policy outcomes of the SCLs initiative. As Stoker (2000) suggests, these new centralised arrangements allowed Government to use institutional power and fiscal control to effect policy change.

The empirical evidence provided in this article suggests that political power was exercised through new structural conditions and relationships imposed upon education and sport agencies involved in the SCLs work strand. Our data suggests that the resource-dependent relationships that exist within the structural arrangements for the SCLs programme are indicative of central Government's desire to exert political control over youth sport policy outcomes in school and community contexts. For the two sports investigated in this study, the funding for the SCLs programme represented a significant income stream and as a consequence DCMS, through Sport England, was able to determine precisely how the funding was spent.

The politicisation of PE and youth sport in England manifests itself in several ways: firstly, the hierarchical, top-down structure of policy delivery exhibits little of the celebrated 'new governance' principles that many commentators describe; secondly, the requirement placed upon agencies in receipt of Government funding to deliver successful centrally-set targets; and thirdly, the threat of withdrawal of that funding if agencies were unsuccessful in achieving their targets. Whilst we acknowledge that any funder would seek a return for their investment, the evidence that emerges from our investigation of the SCLs work strand supports our contention that PE and youth sport policy has become increasingly politicised, tightly managed and controlled. For scholars of sport policy, the 'governance' debate provides a useful lens through which to analyse policy change; however our study has revealed that whilst an array of para-statal bodies are involved in the delivery of PE and youth sport policy, it does not hold that this has led to a dispersal of power and a weakening of central control. On the contrary, 'new' governance arrangements appear paradoxically, to have led to *more* centralised control of PE and youth sport policy.

Note

1 Sport England (2004) identified 20 Priority Sports to make England a successful sporting nation. Each priority sport (as a condition of funding) was required to develop targets for world rankings and performance in sport through their 'whole sport plans', setting targets to achieve the vision for England to be the best sporting nation in the world.

References

Bevir, M. and Rhodes, R.A.W. (2003) *Interpreting British governance.* London: Routledge.

——— (2006) *Governance stories.* London: Routledge.

——— 2008) 'The differentiated polity as narrative', *British Journal of Politics and International Relations* Vol. 10, No. 4: pp. 729–34.

Cabinet Office (1999) *Modernising government. Executive summary.* London: National Audit Office, HMSO.

CCPR (1960) *Sport and the community: The Report of the Wolfenden Committee on Sport.* London: CCPR.

CCPR (2003) Transcript of Richard Caborn's opening speech at CCPR 20 May 2003. http: //www.culture.gov.uk/Reference_library/Minister _Speeches/Richard_Caborn/Richard_Caborn_Speech03.htm (Accessed 24 April, 2007).

Clarke, M and Stewart, J. (1999) *Community governance, community leadership and the new local government.* JRF/YPS: York.

Daily Telegraph (2010) 'The Open 2010: Golf blossoms and provides role model for English sport', Wednesday, 14th July, 2010.

Deem, R. and Brehony, K. J. (2005) 'Management as ideology: The case of "new managerialism" in higher education', *Oxford Review of Education* Vol. 31, No. 2: pp. 217–235.

DfES (2001) *Schools achieving success.* London: HMSO.

——— *A new specialist system: Transforming secondary education.* London: DfES.

DCMS/DfES (2002) *The role of Further and Higher Education in delivering the Government's plan for Sport.* London: DCMS/DfES.

DfES/DCMS (2003) *Learning through PE and Sport. A guide to the Physical Education, School Sport and Club Link Strategy.* London: Department for Education and Skills

England Athletics (2010) *Schools and clubs: Growing the next generation of athletics champions ... together.* http: //www.englandathletics.org/ page.asp?section=587&sectionTitle=Schools+athletics (Accessed 17 September, 2010).

Flintoff, A. (2003) 'The School Sport Co-ordinator Programme: Changing the role of the physical education teacher?', *Sport, Education and Society* Vol. 8, No. 2: pp. 231–250.

Foster, A. (2004) *Moving on. A review of the need for change in athletics in the UK*. Presented to UK Sport and Sport England, May 2004.

Gains, C. (2009) 'Cross country running in 2009', http: //www.british athleticsclubs.com/ (Accessed 25 June, 2009).

Golf Foundation (2004) *Annual Report*. http: //www.golf foundation.org/ index.cfm?id=2 (Accessed 20 September, 2006).

————(2005 *Annual Report*. http: //www.golf foundation.org/index. cfm?id=2 (Accessed 20 September, 2006).

———— (2007) History of the Golf Foundation http: //www.golf-foundation. org/index.cfm?id=39 (14/04/07).

Goodwin, M. and Grix, J. (2011) 'Bringing structures back in: The "governance narrative", the "decentred approach" and "asymmetrical network governance" in the education and sport policy communities', *Public Administration*, in press.

Grix, J. (2010) 'Introducing "hard interpretivism" and "Q" methodology', *Leisure Studies* Vol. 29, No. 4: pp. 457–467.

———— (2010) *Foundations of research* 2nd Edition. Basingstoke: Palgrave.

Grix, J. and Parker, A. (2011 forthcoming) 'Towards an explanation for the decline in UK Athletics: A case study of male distance running', *Sport in Society*.

Grix, J. and Phillpots, L. (2011, forthcoming) 'Revisiting the "governance narrative": "asymmetrical network governance" and the "deviant" case of the sport policy sector', *Public Policy and Administration* Vol. 26, No. 1.

Houlihan, B (2000) 'Sporting excellence, schools and sports development', *European Physical Education Review* Vol. 6, No. 2: pp. 171–194.

Houlihan, B. and Green, M. (2006) 'The changing status of school sport and physical education: Explaining policy change', *Sport, Education and Society* Vol. 11, No. 1: pp. 73–79.

———— (2009) 'Modernisation and sport: The reform of Sport England and UK Sport', *Public Administration* Vol. 87, No. 3: pp. 678–698.

Hylton, K. and Bramham, P. (2007) *Sports development: Policy, process and practice*. London: Routledge.

Orme, D. (2005) 'Why is participation falling?', Association of GB Athletic Clubs: http: //www.britishathleticsclubs.com/ (Accessed: 21 March, 2007).

Phillpots, L. (2007) *An analysis of the policy process for selected elements of the Physical education, school sport and club links strategy in England*, Loughborough, unpublished thesis.

Phillpots, L., Grix, J. with Quarmby, T. (2011) 'Unpacking the paradox: Centralised grass-roots policy and "new Governance": A case study of County Sport Partnerships', *International Review of Sport Sociology* (pre-published online, August, 2010).

Roberts, K. (1996) 'Young people, schools, sport and government policies', *Sport, Education and Society* Vol. 1, No.1: pp. 47–57.

Sanderson, I. (2002), 'Making sense of "what works": Evidence based policy making as instrumental rationality?', *Public Policy and Administration* Vol. 17, No. 3: pp. 61–75.

Skelcher, C. 2000. 'Changing images of the state: Overloaded, hollowed-out, congested', *Public Policy and Administration* Vol. 15, No. 3: pp. 3–19.

Smith, A. and Leech, R. (2010) 'Evidence. What evidence?: Evidence-based policy making and School Sport Partnerships in North West England', *International Journal of Sport Policy* Vol. 2, No. 3: pp. 327–345.

Sport England (2004) *The framework for sport in England: Making England an active and successful sporting nation: A vision for 2020.* London.

—— (2006) *Annual report and accounts.* London: The Stationery Office.

—— (2010) Club Links http://www.sportengland.org/support_advice/children_and_young_people/community _and _club_activities/club_links.aspx (Accessed 31 September, 2010).

Stoker, G (ed) (1999) *The new management of British local government.* Basingstoke: Macmillan.

TNS (2006) School Sport Survey http://www.dfes.gov.uk/rsgateway/DB/RRP/u015000/index.shtml (Accessed 8 August, 2007).

THE ROLE OF ALTERNATIVE PHYSICAL ACTIVITIES IN ENGAGING YOUNG PEOPLE

**Steve Bullough, Gemma Hart,
Richard Moore, Stuart Bonner**

Sport Industry Research Centre,
Sheffield Hallam University

Introduction

The 2009 PE and Sport Strategy for Young People (PESSYP) recognised that all young people have different needs and preferences, which continually change throughout childhood and adolescence (Sport England, 2009a). Research published by Boyle *et al.* (2008) reported that teachers found that engaging external agencies in the provision of extra-curricular clubs, and the provision of alternative physical activities (APAs), encouraged children who would not normally be active to take part. The role of Physical Education in the National Curriculum has developed significantly in the last two decades, particularly since the 1988 curriculum reforms (discussed later). Changes in the National Curriculum have developed alongside an increasing level of support for the delivery of sport through national agencies. This has increased the focus and the provision of extra curricular activities, in particular those delivered by an increasing number and range of agencies outside the traditional school setting. This has been facilitated and progressed through the creation and growth of the school sport networks which were created following policy intervention. This increased range of providers have increased the options for young people to take part and, where activities are delivered in non-traditional settings, played a role in encouraging young people to take part.

Access and exposure to a wide range of activities provides a platform from which young people can develop their tastes and preferences for sport which can be carried on into adulthood. This is not to suggest that traditional sports should be substituted as they

47

remain popular, but it is intended to highlight the need for a balanced blend of options which increase the possibility of engaging with a greater proportion of young people. This applies particularly to those who are put off by the competitive team sports which historically have dominated PE in schools. This access has become increasingly possible through the process, pathways and exit routes which have developed in the last decade through policy interventions in England, for example, the PE, School Sport and Club Links strategy (PESSCL) which was later developed into the PE, School Sport and Young People strategy (PESSYP), which have increased the extra curricular opportunities on offer. This increase in the provision of less mainstream sports within schools, can be demonstrated through the increase in the average number of sports offered per school, which has increased from 14.5 sports in 2003/04 to 17.5 sports in 2007/08 (Department for Children Schools and Families [DCSF], 2008).

As a recent example, there has been considerable national investment into the rising popularity of alternative activities through programmes such as the £36 million 'Sport Unlimited' project, which is funded and managed by the Department for Culture, Media and Sport (DCMS) and Sport England. Alternative activities provided under this programme includes the delivery of initiatives such as the Street Games programme which takes sport to young people in deprived areas and in environments which they are familiar with, to encourage them to take up activity. Popular Alternative Physical Activities (APAs) sit alongside more traditional sports in delivery plans (Sport England, 2008a) which are designed using information from the results from consultations with young people. One of the initial steps in the Sport Unlimited programme was determining what sports young people want to do in terms of establishing a demand for, and the role of, APAs in the programme. The evaluation of years one and two of the Sport Unlimited project has highlighted (through those consultations with young people) that there is a need to provide APAs and to be more creative about how these opportunities are packaged and offered to young people. In many cases Sport Unlimited activities were offered as taster sessions and included adapted versions of more extreme sports. The taster sessions then led into ten week Sport Unlimited programmes before the young people involved were signposted into club based activity so that they could continue to participate further, should they wish. This is particularly important for the Sport Unlimited target group of young people who have often only partially engaged in extra-curricular opportunities provided through both schools and the wider community.

However, determining what constitutes an APA is a key priority in understanding the role that these activities can play in delivering sustained participation. This chapter begins by setting out the background to the National Curriculum, the role of alternative activities in its history and its role in providing opportunities for participation. The paper outlines what constitutes an alternative activity from existing academic theory and discusses where APAs fit within the spectrum of sport and in the context of the National Curriculum. Contextualising what APAs are and where they are positioned in current provision creates a discussion around their importance in engaging young people. An overview of the 'size' of the APA market for adults is presented alongside results for the demand for APAs from young people. Finally, a case study from the Sport Unlimited project is presented to highlight examples of APAs in engaging young people.

The development of the National Curriculum

Records indicate that physical education first appeared in British schools between 1860 and 1880 and was known as 'drill' (Houlihan, 2008), based on a view that children from working-class families needed to be controlled and disciplined (Kirk, 1998). State education content was devised by ex public school boys who had become part of the ruling classes in England, which meant that it was therefore inevitable that public school athleticism would become the basis for PE in state schools (Love, 2007). The main focus of athleticism was physical exercise and team games (Mangan, 2010), however the influence of public schools led to swimming being introduced within state schools via the Education Department between the 1870s and 1918 (Love, 2007). The physical education syllabus was published in 1933 and lasted for twenty years until the early fifties. The view that PE was a release from the classroom has been fought ever since, particularly in the face of a decreasing allocation of time within schools (Houlihan, 2008). In the post-war years of the 20th century, PE was very much focused on the areas of gymnastics, games and athletics. Keighley (1993) suggested that Outdoor Adventure Activities (OAA) were generally accessible for young people via the Outward Bound movement and Youth Associations, such as the Scout movement, and that it wasn't until the 1950s that OAA began to find an important place in both the formal curriculum and extra-curriculum of many schools.

A major event in the development of physical education was the Education Reform Act of 1988, which saw the introduction of the National Curriculum for Physical Education (NCPE) in England and Wales (Houlihan, 2008). The NCPE has been revised several times between 1995 and 2010. Currently there are six areas of the National Curriculum: games; athletics; gymnastics; dance; outdoor adventure activities; and swimming/water safety (Honeybourne *et al.*, 2004). Prior to 1988 there was little provision for individualised or minority sports in schools. Houlihan (as cited in Evans *et al.*, 1996) outlined the government ideology for how PE should be positioned in the curriculum. The main debate surrounded whether the traditional view which focuses on competitive team sport should be the model or a focus on more innovative and inclusive approach to physical education (Houlihan, 2008; Evans, 1990). History outlines that the traditionalist ideology was adopted which, according to Penney and Evans (1999) has denied access to a broader blend of balanced experiences through PE. Research undertaken in the 1990s by Evans *et al.* (1996) and Penney and Evans (1999) suggests that the introduction of the National Curriculum has not resulted in any diverse or new approach to physical education but has "consolidated marginality".

Alternative activities in the National Curriculum

The increased role of sport in the National Curriculum and extra curricular provision has seen a shift from skills-based sports and physical activity, to more holistic learning and emphasis on encouraging lifelong participation (Green, 2002). This has led to an increased demand and attention for so called 'lifestyle' activities, as opposed to the more traditional skills-based activities, with the aim of promoting lifelong participation in physical activity (Green, 2002). The 'yoUR Activity toolkit', which was devised by the Youth Sport Trust in 2009, is an example of support for the provision of 'alternative activities and modified traditional sports' for young people in Key Stage 4 (KS4) who were disengaged from exercise, sport and physical activity. The integration of wider themes into the National Curriculum to sit alongside the more traditional themes is an example of the wider focus. However, there was still a disparity in the themes of sport offered in school, as shown in the 2002 Sport England young people survey (discussed in greater detail below). Bloyce and Smith (2010) highlighted that it is important to bear in mind that, for many young people, more individualistic and flexible activities dominate their leisure-sport and physical activity lifestyles; and Roberts (1996) comments that these are activities that they prefer to take part in, in their own time, with their own friends. In terms of understanding the range of activities and focus of the curriculum, it is worth noting that five of the six themes in the National Curriculum are compulsory throughout all four key stages and this allows a wide range of activities to be delivered until the age of 16. Swimming, however, is the one exception as it is compulsory until the end of Key Stage 2 only (or 11 years old) and does not have to be offered in secondary schools.

The expansion of extra curricular sport

In the last decade, the investment in extra curricular sport has been developed through targeted strategies by national agencies. This coincided with official targets for the amount of time PE should be allocated within the Curriculum (Houlihan, 2008). The original PESSCL strategy enabled the UK government to invest in sporting programmes through specialist sports colleges and National Governing Bodies (NGBs) in order to increase mass participation in physical activity and also to assist with the identification of the nation's most talented children (Hylton'and Bramham, 2007). This led to the introduction of the Physical Education Sport Strategy for Young People (PESSYP) which aimed to build on the successes of the PESSCL strategy and to provide 5–16 year olds with two hours of high quality PE in schools and three hours of physical activity outside of school. The 'five hour offer' was an ambitious target and the previous Labour government stated that it was only possible if PE, school and club sport work together throughout the local community in order to promote physical activity (Youth Sport Trust, 2009). It has also been reported that this strategy has had a large impact on physical education provision, with the selection of strands available increasing, which enables participation to widen in community club and after school sports activities (OFSTED, 2009).

The debate outlined by Penney and Evans (1999), between traditional approaches to delivering sport in schools and a broader, more balanced approach, continues in the modern era. It has been suggested that schools incorporating non-traditional, aesthetic or leisure-based activities within their provision will encourage and motivate young people to participate, especially if traditional team activities do not attract them (OFSTED, 2009). It has also been stated that approximately one third of schools recognised the need to personalise their provision and that such innovative practice was enriching school PE and enabling students to request activities that were reducing disaffection, leading to improvements in engagement, especially among vulnerable groups (OFSTED, 2009).

However, the incumbent coalition government outlined plans in the October 2010 Comprehensive Spending Review to cut the commitment to 'ring fenced' funding for the School Sport Partnership (SSP) network, with all funding from the government put into mainstream school budgets, not specific subject areas (HM Treasury, 2010). The rationale behind this is that local schools should be able to allocate their own resources and fund extra curricular sports themselves should they see its value. A major change in sport policy for young people since the change in government (2010) is the increased focus on the role of competition (Department for Education, 2010), as demonstrated by the decision to only provide formal funding in the form of a 'School games competition'. This has been met with opposition from the previous Labour government (who implemented the PESSCL and PESSYP strategies which increased the focus on PE and extra curricular sport through the five hour offer) which has created further debate. Part of the rationale for opposition follows the same argument outlined by Penney and Evans (1993). Although competition is a vital part of delivering successful sport programmes, a blend of activities which appeal to as many young people as possible is required if wider engagement is to be achieved. It can be argued that those young people who do not want to take part in competitive (and predominantly team) sports should still be provided with curricular and extra-curricular opportunities. Furthermore, there is an argument to be made that it is not possible for every school to find a place in a competitive team for every child.

Academic theory on alternative activities

Wheaton (2010: p. 1057) noted an increase in academic interest in the field of what has been "variously labelled alternative, new, extreme, adventure, panic, action, whiz and lifestyle sport". This interest not only includes research which has contributed to the significance of such alternative sporting activities, their cultures and identities, but also understanding the relationships between sport and society more widely. It has been suggested that it is hard to assess or calculate participation rates of alternative activities due to the roving nature of such activities and the informal and counter-cultural context of the sports (Tomlinson et al., 2005; Wheaton, 2010). However, from its inception in 2006, the Sport England Active People Survey (APS) has quantified adult participation (over 16) in England for a wide range of activities including APAs. Furthermore, the 2002 Young People and Sport survey from Sport England and the PESSYP surveys have begun to assess engagement in sport for young people. The Sport Unlimited programme has also consulted with young people to assess their demand for sport for young people (Bullough, Hart and Gregory, 2011). Wheaton (2010) cites sources such as equipment sales, market research and media commentaries as evidence of growth in APAs, although participation statistics from the APS can be used to complement or dispute these figures. Notwithstanding this, Wheaton suggests that alternative activities are seeing accelerated expansion in popularity when compared to traditional sports. It is also argued that this expansion of popularity is not confined to young males but includes females and older adults, and that participation can translate from taster sessions through to 'hard core practitioners'.

The development of academic thinking has increased knowledge around the subject, with publications on APAs adding to the more traditional forums of informal discussion, through the printed media (magazines) and online. Furthermore, this growth has expanded into the many courses available to study alternative activity practices through Higher and Further Education. This point is illustrated by the admissions guide from the University and Colleges Admissions Service (UCAS, 2010) for courses starting in 2011. This indicated 51 courses at 30 different institutions for 'outdoor-related' qualifications (in November 2010). This is a development on the supply side which, through increasing the quantity and quality of specialist trained practitioners, helps to create and facilitate some of the formal delivery, including the provision for young people. At present this occurs through existing networks, such as County Sport Partnerships (CSPs), Community Sport Networks (CSNs) and Community Sport and Physical Activity Networks (CSPANs) which were created by changes in policy over the last decade and facilitate programmes like Sport Unlimited.

What are Alternative Physical Activities (APAs)?

The definition of APAs is rather ambiguous. Rinehart and Sydnor (2003) have offered a definition they say covers a wide range of activities, or anything that doesn't fit under the categories in western sport. This is reaffirmed by Thorpe and Rinehart (2010) who outline that APAs are unlike traditional sports which can be highly regulated and regimented. Wheaton (2010) however expresses some concern over the labelling of activities as 'alternative' or 'extreme' because the term 'alternative' is applied as a wider-ranging term as well as to a set of activities; and 'extreme' is a misleading term driven by the media. Booth and Thorpe (2007) also dislike the term 'extreme', reporting that many activities which are given this label are in fact very safe. It is acknowledged that some extreme sports, if carried out in unsafe, unsupervised and uncontrolled environments and without the appropriate equipment, could be very dangerous. However as Wheaton (2010) rightly highlights, many of these sports do not carry any more risk than some of the more traditional sports such as swimming and football if conducted appropriately.

A number of authors (Coalter, 1996; Tomlinson *et al.* 2005; Wheaton, 2004) use the term 'lifestyle sports' as a substitute for the term 'alternative activities'. The term 'lifestyle sports' encompasses much more than just the name or type of sport; often lifestyle sports indicate a 'way of life'. Lifestyle, as reported by Tomlinson *et al.* (2005), is a self-interpreted pattern of actions that differentiates one person from another. Lifestyle sports can contribute to this through interpretations of how people look and behave, and it is through these activities that people can interact, sharing tastes and interests and creating a sense of belongingness. While motives for getting started in the sport tended to be interpersonal (e.g. friends asked them to try it) and hedonic (e.g. the desire for 'thrills'), maintenance of involvement was motivated by a combination of the desire to achieve mastery and status and the opportunity to construct a new personal identity. Skiing, for example, has been described as a lifestyle sport (Coalter, 1996; Wheaton, 2004) as it is an activity which is individual and flexible, and can be non-competitive as well as fitness-oriented.

Activities such as skiing represent not only a form of sporting participation but also a form of social engagement: Wheaton (2004) reported that such activities may be attractive to people who have been alienated by traditional school-based activities and institutionalised sport practices. Thorpe and Rinehart (2010) suggest that such activities are more likely to be lived in the moment and that individuals taking part in these activities are likely to resist any adherence to rigid rules. Midol and Broyer (1995) also support this idea, and suggest that activities such as windsurfing, surfing, snowboarding and skateboarding are playful practices grounded in the 'here and now', and generally lack the element of competition. In determining motivation for participation, Hellison *et al.* (2000, p. 67) suggest that "many youngsters desire alternative activities that provide excitement, challenge and a degree of risk". Coakley (2004) suggests that a primary reason why young people participate in extreme sports is because there is no authority figure in charge of their participation. Beal's research on skateboarding (as cited in Yiannakis and Melnick, 2001 p. 54) provides one skateboarder's insight on competition, reinforcing the cooperative nature of some lifestyle sports: "we don't have to skate against anybody, we skate with them".

Self-discovery, as well as escape, is a feature of these activities and participants can gain a sense of achievement, which can ultimately boost their confidence (Mintel, 2003).

Thorpe and Rinehart (2010) highlighted that alternative sports often involve a special relationship with the natural environment. Such relationships can be quite different from formalised sports where play takes place on artificial, formally constituted spaces such as courts, arenas, fields and tracks. Willig (2008) also suggested that continued participation in APA is less about pleasure and more about the challenge. This supports Colaizzi (as cited in Willig, 2008, p. 694) who stated, "the knowledge that one's activities are too challenging for most people to contemplate does contribute to their attraction ... taking part in these activities constitutes an extremely important part of one's life and that one's sense of self, identity and well-being is clearly bound up with them".

Summary of the APA definitions

It is evident that there are varying definitions for the term 'alternative physical activities', but despite this it is clear that the term encompasses an array of non-traditional sports away from the mainstream. These often include sports which have an element of adventure and thrill. It is clear that, for many, participation in APAs, or lifestyle sports, is an important part of their social engagement with others. The flexible and laid-back focus that characterises important elements of APAs also appear to be a significant attraction to the sports.

Policy

Prior to Tomlinson *et al.'s* (2005) commissioned work, no previous research by academics or policy analysts had focused on lifestyle sport and its implications for national sport policy. Sport policy in England has set ambitious targets for physical activity and sport participation as outlined in the Game Plan (2002), DCMS (2002), as well as Sport England's strategy (2008b) which has three main objectives ('Grow', 'Sustain' and 'Excel').

It has been suggested that the achievability of targets is very much dependent on the ability to understand and adapt to change within the sports sector (Tomlinson *et al.*, 2005). Concentrating solely on traditional forms of sport may not lead to the growth in participation required to hit targets set out in the Grow, Sustain and Excel strategy (2008–11). In this context, recognising the diversity of sport cultures and practices that exist outside of traditional sport provision has become increasingly important to policy analysts. Tomlinson *et al.* (2005) suggests that in terms of the research agenda for Sport England, the central finding is that rather than the traditional emphasis on individual sports, data collection with respect to lifestyle sports needs to focus on the participants. They suggest that these sports are very much an expression of their identities and lifestyles rather than existing as institutionalised forms in their own right.

There have been significant developments in market segment-ation through the Sport England administered Active People Survey, the DCMS administered Taking Part Survey and the Mosaic tool from . Experian. Nineteen segments have been identified (Sport England, 2010b) and provide an excellent tool to create a greater understanding of the segments where APA participants are most likely to come from which can help to inform policy in the future. The development of market segments allows practitioners to understand participants (and non-participants) in much greater detail. This includes their motiva-tions, the barriers faced by such segments, their satisfaction with their existing sporting experience, the other activities they enjoy, pre-ferred brands and the types of media channels which are most likely to reach particular segments.

Coakley and White (1992) argue that if the goal of leisure pro-vision is to provide only what young people have had the opportu-nities to experience in the past then raising participation in activity may not be achieved. Care and sensitivity are needed in order to provide young people with opportunities to raise questions and move beyond what has traditionally been available and accepted. Alter-native activities within the school PE environment are becoming increasingly popular (Kirk, 2005) as the education system is begin-ning to understand that more positive experiences of school PE may encourage further participation later in life or even a more positive attitude to taking part in PE lessons, a point which was echoed by Coakley and White (1992).

School Sport Partnerships were set up in 2000 (Sport England 2009a) with the aim of bringing families of schools together in order to enhance sports opportunities for young people and develop stra-tegic links with key partners in sport and the wider community as part of the PE School Sport and Young People Strategy (formerly the PE School Sport and Club Links Strategy). Considerable progress has been made in terms of raising participation rates in PE and Sport as highlighted in the 2009/10 School Sport Survey. Over a period of seven years (the first school sport survey was undertaken in 2003/04), the provision of sports increased from an average of 14 sports in the 2003/04 survey to an average of 19 sports in the 2009/10 survey. This included the provision of APAs such as canoeing, rowing, martial arts and archery, all of which had risen at least ten percentage points over the seven years. The percentage of young people participating in community sports, dance or multi-skills clubs had also risen over the seven year period. The contribution that School Sport Partnerships have made and committed to increasing this provision has had 'some impact' (Loughborough Partnership, 2005, 2006; Office for Standards in Education [OFSTED], 2003, 2004, 2005), particularly in relation to increasing community clubs links and providing opportunities for young people to take part in alternative activities. This has been achieved by forging partnerships with external deliverers in order to provide the skill level needed to deliver such activities. The Sport Unlimited project has also had a key role in facilitating this with a wide range of partnerships created throughout the programme allowing a variety of opportunities to be offered to young people.

Schools have been acknowledged as the institution with primary responsibility for promoting activities to young people and, more specifically, school PE has been recognised as having a big role to play (Cale and Harris, 2006). Schools have implemented the use of APAs within the National Curriculum which have allowed them to grow, starting at grassroots and working up through lifelong participation. As Roberts (1999) suggests, the introduction of a broader spectrum of activities will allow young people to make their own decisions about what they will do and how they will do it.

Categorising sports — what sports are 'alternative activities'?

In order to demonstrate the role of APAs in engaging young people it is necessary to understand the context of the National Curriculum in the UK as this provides a base/starting point of demand (in regard to tastes and preferences). When analysing 'types of activity', it is possible to categorise sports into the themes set out in the National Curriculum — games; athletics; gymnastics; dance; outdoor adventure activities; and swimming/water safety. Categorising sports allows authorities to understand how the six themes can be offered through programmes aimed at increasing engagement in sport.This categorisation of sports outlines the volume of APAs for potential participation.

Every sport, despite potentially exhibiting similar characteristics to other sports, is not homogenous in terms of the way it is enacted. Furthermore, individual sports are not homogenous in terms of the demand for them and, in many aspects, the supply of them. With the increasing body of knowledge about the characteristics of individuals participating in alternative activities (through Active People data and the market segmentation profiles), it would be false to suggest that

young people can be separated into homogenous groups based on their demand for activities as either a 'traditional' or an 'alternative' participant. Tastes and preferences, particularly for young people, can change quickly (Mulvihill *et al.*, 2000), and there will be overlap in the demand for traditional activities and alternative activities.

Since the NCPE revision in 1999, schools are required to work with the six categories of activities (Armour and Kirk, as cited in Houlihan, 2008). This allows authorities to recognise where activities which are categorised as 'alternative' are positioned in the overall spectrum of sports participation. This also highlights the importance of alternative activities in engaging young people, particularly in developing programmes on the supply side. Although the tastes and preferences for sport from young people change and develop, it can be argued that providing the opportunity to be introduced to as many activities from an early age is important in engaging young people, particularly those who may not engage with traditional activities. This is a key objective of the Sport Unlimited project. In order to categorise sports, we have started at the base of participation (the National Curriculum) to put sports into context with the area which has seen a significant investment in terms of policy over the last decade. In 2007 Sport England presented a list in which the organisation recognised 105 'sports'; this was extended in 2010 to a list of 147 recognised sports (Sport England, 2010a), and suggested these as the "activities home country sports councils may wish to work with and the organisations which govern those activities". Furthermore, Sport England outlined 46 'funded sports' between 2009 and 2013 (Sport England, 2009b). When examining this list, it appeared prudent to link this list with the guidelines set out in the National Curriculum for physical education, so as to understand sports as part of existing classifications. We have applied this list from Sport England in **Table 1**, which also outlines where we have placed the 147 sports into the six National Curriculum categories. The 46 'funded sports for 2009–2013' are in bold.

It is evident that generally the term APAs encompasses non traditional sporting activities which often incorporate an element of adventure. Those sports in the 'outdoor and adventure' category in **Table 1** align as the "best fit" with the definition of APAs from the available academic theory. There are a few caveats when applying this method which need to be outlined. Certain sports which could be classified as combat sports — for example, Boxing and Martial Arts — do not really fit in the National Curriculum themes. Although combat sports are not traditionally offered through curricular PE, they have

Table 1	Categorisation of 147 sports into the six National Curriculum categories

Category	Sports
GAMES	American Football, **Association Football**, Australian Rules Football, **Badminton**, **Baseball and Softball***, **Basketball**, Bicycle Polo, Billiards, **Boccia**, **Bowls**, Camogie, **Cricket**, Croquet, Curling, Darts, Dodgeball, Fives, Floorball, Futsal, Gaelic Football, **Goalball**, **Golf**, **Handball**, Hockey and Puck (Roller), **Hockey**, Hurling, Ice Hockey, Kabaddi, Korfball, **Lacrosse**, **Lawn Tennis**, **Netball**, Octopush, Petanque, Polo, Polocrosse, Pool, Quoits, Racketball, Rackets, Real Tennis, **Rounders**, **Rugby League**, **Rugby Union**, Shinty, Snooker, **Squash**, Stoolball, **Table Tennis**, Tenpin Bowling, Ultimate (Frisbee), **Volleyball**, Water Polo.
GYMNASTICS	**Gymnastics**, Trampolining, Yoga
ATHLETICS	Arm Wrestling, **Athletics**, Biathlon, **Cycling**, Duathlon, Exercise and Fitness, Health and Beauty Exercise, Keep Fit, **Modern Pentathlon**, Powerlifting, **Rowing**, Skipping, **Triathlon**, Tug of War, **Weightlifting**, **Wrestling**.
DANCE	Ballroom Dancing, Baton Twirling, Dance Sport, Folk Dancing, **Movement and Dance**.

OUTDOOR AND ADVENTURE
(*classified in this paper as 'Alternative Activities'*)

Aikido, **Angling**, **Archery**, Artistic Skating (roller), Ballooning, BMX, Bobsleigh, **Boxing**, **Canoeing**, Caving, Chinese Martial Arts, Clay Pigeon Shooting, Dragon Boat Racing, **Equestrian**, **Fencing**, Flying, Gliding, Hangliding and Paragliding, Harness Racing, Highland Games, Horse Racing, Horse Riding, Hovering, Ice Skating, Jet Skiing, Ju Jitsu, **Judo**, Karate, Kendo, Kite Surfing, Kneeboarding, Land-Sailing/Yachting, Luge, Model Aircraft Flying, Motor Cruising, Motor Cycling, Motor Sports, Mountain Biking, **Mountaineering**, **Orienteering**, Parachuting, Powerboating, Rafting, Rambling, Roller Sports, **Sailing** and Yachting, Sand and Land Yachting, **Shooting**, Show Jumping, Skateboarding, Skater Hockey (Roller), **Skiing****, **Snowboarding****, Sombo, Speed Skating (Roller), Speedway, Surfing, **Taekwondo**, Tang Soo Do, Wakeboarding, **Water Skiing**, Windsurfing.

SWIMMING/WATER SAFETY

Aquathlon, Diving, Life Saving, Sub Aqua, Surf Life Saving, **Swimming**.

NB: "Disability Sport" is the 147th sport, but is not included due to the ambiguity of the activity title. Wheelchair Basketball and Wheelchair Rugby are the 45th and 46th funded sports.

* "Baseball/Softball" and "Softball" are two entries on the list of 147

** "Skiing/Snowboarding" are two sports on the overall list of 147 and one sport on the funded list.

a significant and increasing presence in extra-curricular sport for young people, in particular through the modified versions used in taster sessions through Sport Unlimited. There are some sports which are placed outside of the 'outdoor and adventure' (alternative activities) theme which could, however, cross over and also be categorised as an 'alternative activity'. These activities are presented in **Table 2**, which are in addition to the alternative activities already in the 'outdoor and adventure' category, as described above. Despite these sports not being 'outdoor and adventure' activities, they are classified as 'alternative' in the context of Sport Unlimited (in the PESSYP policy) and could therefore be placed in that category. Furthermore, there are some sports which cross over categories: for example, rowing could be "outdoor" on a river, or "athletic" on a rowing machine. There are also a small proportion of sports which are included in the Active People surveys but are not on this list"— e.g. abseiling and snorkelling.

Having categorised sports into the six curriculum themes it is possible to highlight the role Sport Unlimited has had in promoting and delivering APAs, and why they are important in the scope of increasing participation. **Table 3** shows a summary of Table 1 and outlines the proportion of the 147 sports which fit in to each theme, the number of sports which are 'funded' by Sport England and the number of those sports offered by Sport Unlimited in eight full terms of delivery.

It is interesting that, of the 146 sports on the list, alternative activities account for 62 (or 42%). Furthermore, 14 of these activities are part of the 46 funded sports for 2009–2013 (or 30% of funded sports). This categorisation highlights the significant proportion of activities which are 'alternative' and outlines the importance of variety in shaping provision for young people, particularly through extra curricular programmes as part of the five hour offer. Sport Unlimited, in its first two years, has offered 85 sports on the list (or 58%) and 91% of the Sport England funded sports. Sport Unlimited has also offered 29 of 62 sports (47%) of the APAs on the list and 12 out of 14 (87%) of the funded sports. This percentage would also increase if certain sports which are unlikely to be provided in extra curricular options were omitted from the calculation: for example, flying, dragon boat racing and motor sport.

Table 2	Sports which could also cross over as an 'alternative activity'

Category	Sports
Games	American Football, Australian Rules Football, Bicycle Polo, **Boccia**, **Bowls**, Camogie, Croquet, Curling, Dodgeball, Fives, Floorball, Futsal, Gaelic Football, **Goalball**, **Handball**, Hockey and Puck (Roller), Hurling, Ice Hockey, Kabaddi, Korfball, Octopush, Petanque, Polo, Polocrosse, Quoits, Racketball, Rackets, Real Tennis, Shinty, Stoolball, Tenpin Bowling, Ultimate (Frisbee), Water Polo
Gymnastics	Trampolining
Athletics	**Modern Pentathlon**, **Rowing**, **Wrestling**
Dance	**Movement and Dance** (variations of, e.g. street dance).
Swimming / Water Safety	Aquathlon, Sub Aqua

Table 3	Number of sports offered through Sport Unlimited by theme

Category	No. sports in list of 147	No. activities offered by Sport Unlimited	No. of funded sports	No. of funded sports offered by Sport Unlimited
Games	54	35 (65%)	20	19 (95%)
Gymnastics	3	3 (100%)	1	1 (100%)
Athletics	16	9 (56%)	7	6 (86%)
Dance	5	4 (80%)	1	1 (100%)
Outdoor and Adventure ('Alternative Activities')	62	29 (47%)	14[b]	12 (86%)
Swimming / Water Safety	6	5 (83%)	1	1 (100%)
OVERALL	146[a]	85 (58%)	44[c]	40 (91%)

[a] "Disability Sport" is the 147th sport but is not included in a theme
[b] "Skiing/Snowboarding" are two sports on the overall list of 147 and one sport on the funded list
[c] "Wheelchair Rugby" and "Wheelchair Basketball" are the 45th and 46th funded sports

Engagement in alternative activities

As the collection of participation data for adults has expanded through Active People there has also been investment, although not to the same extent, in surveys for young people, for example, the 2002 Sport England survey, the series of PESSYP surveys and the 'Tellus' surveys. The findings from the 2002 Sport England survey, which outlined the participation in and out of school by the National Curriculum themes, are shown in **Table 4**. The themes are the six National Curriculum themes although 'gymnastics' and 'athletics' were merged.

The data in **Table 4** was collected prior to the substantial development of school sport, led by the SSP infrastructure during the last decade, and as a result it is possible that the balance of activities has changed. Notwithstanding this, Table 4 shows that almost all young people surveyed (99%) had taken part in sport in school at least once and 98% of young people had taken part at least once outside of school. However, participation by theme highlights some differences between participation in school and out of school. In school, games (93%) and gymnastics/athletics (92%) were the themes where the majority of engagement had occurred. Less than half had taken part in 'swimming/water safety' in school (48%) and around a third had taken part in 'outdoor/adventure' (37%) and dance (30%). This is contrasted by participation out of school which, in the case of swimming, almost doubled, and alternative/outdoor activities, which more than doubled. Although the engagement is still dominated by 'games' (91%), the results show that 'outdoor/adventure' was the second highest theme in terms of engagement out of school (84%) compared to fourth in school. Engagement with 'dance' was also higher outside of school. This survey took place just before the publication of the original PESSCL strategy, launched in 2002 (DCMS, 2002b), which has provided a wider network of opportunities; the figures for 2002 suggest that the policies which were designed to promote alternative

Table 4   *Engagement in sport according to the 2002 'Young People and Sport' survey*

Category	In School	Out of School
Games	93%	91%
Gymnastics and Athletics (Merged)	92%	77%
Dance	30%	39%
Outdoor and Adventure / APAs	37%	84%
Swimming / Water Safety	48%	80%
Overall engagement in at least one sport	**99%**	**98%**

activities were well placed. Furthermore, the 2008/09 PE and Sport Survey (2009) outlined that, of the 42 sports on the list which had been participated in at school, nine would be classified as alternative (outdoor/adventure, 64%; orienteering, 61%; canoeing, 28%; archery, 25%; mountaineering, 11%; sailing, 11%; equestrian, 5%; angling, 3%; and, skateboarding 3%). The engagement with those nine sports was mixed compared to the sports offered most frequently (football, 96%; dance, 95% and athletics, 93%) and the sports offered least (judo, 1%; kabaddi, 2%; and, goalball, 2%).

The demand for APAs — adults and young people

So far the paper has looked to identify the increasing role of APAs through the National Curriculum and as part of the extra curricular 'five hour offer'. It is, however, also important to understand where the demand for APAs is placed in the context of adult participation alongside young people. Where comparable data is available, **Table 5** highlights the number of people participating in APAs (16+) from Active People 3, next to 'sport to do more of' from the Sport Unlimited student consultation results. Although the results from the Sport Unlimited consultations do not show participation rates, the results

Table 5   *Participation in APAs from Active People 3*

Once a month participation	Active People 3 (2008/9) 16+		Active People 3 (2008/9) 16–19		Sport Unlimited (Sport to do more of) 11–19	
	%	(n)	%	(n)	%	(n)
England Population	16+	41.43m	16–19	2.68m	11–19	5.74m
Angling	0.66%	277,200	0.30%	8,049	3.20%	183,731
Archery	0.14%	58,600	0.30%	8,049	14.60%	838,274
Canoeing and Kayaking	0.35%	146,500	0.80%	21,464	8.80%	505,261
Climbing*	0.03%	10,800	0.90%	24,147	12.70%	729,183
Equestrian	1.02%	425,900	3.00%	80,490	14.10%	809,566
Fencing	0.05%	20,200	0.20%	5,366	8.20%	470,811
Ice Skating	0.17%	69,600	0.60%	16,098	21.30%	1,222,961
Mountaineering	0.55%	228,200	0.90%	24,147	0.001%	57
Orienteering	0.02%	9,300	0.10%	2,683	0.002%	115
Sailing	0.42%	175,000	0.50%	13,415	4.70%	269,855
Shooting	0.26%	109,400	0.30%	8,049	0.001%	115
Skateboarding	0.15%	63,000	0.70%	18,781	6.90%	396,170
Snowsport	0.39%	164,700	0.40%	10,732	12.40%	711,958

* Climbing is not included in the list of 147 sports

from five consultations with young people (n = 60,174) outline the sports they want to do more of. This can be converted into a proportion of 11 to 19 year olds in England using population statistics from the Office for National Statistics (ONS, 2010). Although the age ranges overlap, Table 5 is designed to outline an indicative illustration of the 'size of the market'. Table 5 also shows that, for the thirteen sports where comparable data is available, twelve had a higher participation rate for 16–19 year olds than the national figure (with archery the exception). This is not surprising given that participation decreases with age (as shown in each edition of the General Household Survey from 1971–2003 and Active People from 2006–present), but it does suggest that some of the alternative activities are more popular with the generation of young people who have been exposed to the additional extra curricular options available in the last decade. The increase in supply is important for APAs as catering for many of them requires an availability of facilities and equipment which programmes like Sport Unlimited have provided.

There are caveats to the idea that a young person's current desire to "do more of" a particular sport will translate into sustained participation in that (or any such) activity in adulthood. These include access to appropriate facilities, access to equipment, time pressures and the availability of suitable programmes with pathways and exit routes. However, the presence of such demand should be noted when designing programmes which introduce young people into sport, particularly those who do not engage with the more traditional options. It would not be prudent to assume such reporting of demand and calculation of wider population figures is attainable, due to the many intricacies involved in the demand for leisure. For example, Grainger-Jones (1999) suggested that leisure tastes and preferences can fluctuate rapidly, particularly with young people. The demand for leisure is also seasonal; cyclical; fickle; impacted upon by external events; increasingly articulated through the media; and, relates to a diverse customer base (Grainger-Jones, 1999). All these factors could be in play for participants in APAs (or new experiences) which may follow trends or fashions which are always evolving.

However, it could also be argued that the way alternative activities integrate into the leisure time of young people is, in certain circumstances, different from traditional sports. The informal nature of some alternative sports is part of the attraction, contrasting with the more structured, competitive nature of traditional sports. There is also an additional set of externalities at the micro level which are interesting for APAs. Assessing the demand for leisure involves a concept known as the 'parent demand function'. In this the quantity demanded is measured by the participation rate (Gratton and Taylor, 2000). In addition to the parent demand function, the demand for sport involves subsidiary items such as facilities, equipment and clothing. These are known as 'derived demands', many of which are necessities in order to be able to take part in an activity. A lack of them can, in certain instances, be a barrier to participation. It could be argued, however, that certain derived demands are part of the attraction, particularly for certain age groups for some of the APAs.

Gratton and Taylor (2000) cited the demand for badminton as an example of derived demands. Based on an individual having 'parent demand' to take part, the individual will require the following: a racket, a shuttlecock, clothing and footwear; she/he will also have to pay for rental of court space, someone to play with or against and any associated travel for a return journey to the facility. Using the example of an APA (skiing), an individual would require (to be a participant): skis, poles, helmet, boots, goggles, ski clothing, gloves and have to pay to access a slope. This is an interesting concept for certain alternative activities (e.g. skiing, skateboarding, BMX, sailing) because it could be argued that the derived demands themselves (particularly equipment and clothing) are a significant part of the attraction of the lifestyle which surrounds participation. This includes taking an interest in and purchasing the latest equipment and accessories, and an association with certain brands. Downward *et al.* (2009) suggested that sport clothing has a fashion value which makes them attractive. It can be the case that the clothing and equipment are a big part of the attraction for 'lifestyle' activities, particularly amongst teenagers.

The final part of this paper presents a short case study from the Sport Unlimited programme.

Alternative physical activities in Sport Unlimited: A case study

Sport Unlimited was designed to increase physical activity levels for children and young people who have some interest in sport but participate infrequently, termed 'semi-sporty'. Since the programme began in 2008, APAs have been delivered alongside traditional activities via ten-week taster sessions aimed at young people aged 11 to 19. Overall, 622,362 participants had taken part in the programme by the end of year two, and APAs have proved a popular choice for many young people, with over one hundred variations and adaptations of APAs offered throughout the country, since the programme began. Examples of alternative physical activity provided in this case study include those activities not traditionally offered within the school curriculum. Some existing APAs, which are not currently included on the Sport England list (e.g. dodgeball and stoolball), have benefited from the funding and promotional platform provided by Sport Unlimited. Furthermore, new APAs (e.g. freestyle tennis and street cheer) have been created in response to ideas drawn from consultations with young people, initiated through Sport Unlimited.

The demand for APAs was identified from consultations undertaken with young people and used to design options for ten-week activity blocks. Analysis of five consultations with four County Sport Partnerships were undertaken with the Sport Unlimited evaluation team (in South London 2008, 2009; West London, 2009; Norfolk, 2009; and Tyne and Wear, 2009) and, when calculated, involved 60,174 young people (aged 11–18, or year 7 to year 13). **Table 6** shows the number of young people who were consulted within each County Sport Partnership.

Table 6   Number of young people consulted by County Sport Partnership

County Sport Partnership	Number of participants
Norfolk	23,295
West London	9,559
South London (1)	23,610
South London (2)	2,865
Tyne and Wear*	845

Although the consultations were designed and reported back on a local level only, cumulative results across the consultations found that 40% of the top ten sports chosen by males and females would be classified as an APA. Popular APAs chosen from these consultations includes ice skating, boxing, BMX, horse riding, skiing and climbing. Interestingly, preferences differed for each of these consultations according to gender, age and location.

Parkour, a derivative of free running, is an example of an APA delivered throughout the country which includes vaults and other acrobatics, utilising existing gymnastics equipment and coaches. The West of England Sports Trust delivered free running in year one, attended by 90 young people. They currently attract 50 regular participants per week in a club setting, tailored to different ability levels. Free running is categorised as an extreme and urban activity which differs from mainstream school provision, although other activities which originate from traditional activities have also proved popular with young people. For example, dance-based activities including cheerleading and street dance have helped to boost female participation through Sport Unlimited. Carrick Dance, a cheerleading programme in Cornwall, was delivered across five secondary schools with over 120 young people competing at competition level and 163 children participating in over 60% of sessions. Furthermore, the number of sports on offer to young people in Cornwall had almost doubled in year two from 15 to 29 (which included 14 alternative activities). The alternative activities achieved a year one average retention rate of 89% compared with 92% overall and a 95% retention rate in year two compared to 87% overall. This suggests that, in Cornwall, alternative activities are matching traditional activities in terms of retention.

The deliverers of traditional sports have also adapted their provision to appeal to young people's activity preferences who may not engage with the traditional format. Derivatives of football, rugby, tennis and cricket include 'futsal', 'fit rugby', 'freestyle tennis' and 'kwik cricket'. 'Freestyle tennis', for instance, which is an alternative to the traditional game of tennis because it is purely a skill or tricks-based activity using a tennis ball and a racket to create different skill moves by manipulating the ball in various ways. Similar activities focus on a participant's development of fundamental skills, which can often be applied to the traditional sport version. CSPs have indicated that participants of modified versions of sports are then signposted to traditional sports clubs utilising their existing club networks, should they want to continue. Conversely, other activities like futsal (a five-a-side version of 11–a-side football) are sports with existing competition networks where participants are able to play or compete at an organised level that provides additional opportunities for sustained participation.

An example of how Sport Unlimited has facilitated opening-up the supply of activities is through outdoor/adventure activities, which are inaccessible to many children because of the high cost, and lack of available facilities and supervisory expertise required. This has proved popular with young children seeking new experiences. Rowing sessions, which have been delivered at the Longridge Outdoor Adventure Centre in Buckinghamshire, engaged 102 young people in 2010 and retained 83 participants in the rowing club after the ten-week taster sessions. Two rowers who took up the sport during year one of Sport Unlimited have excelled and have since joined local clubs aiming to be selected to represent Great Britain in junior trials. Longridge have also delivered other APAs with over 60 young people experiencing climbing and 280 young people attending kayaking sessions during 2010. Furthermore, the throughput numbers to the centre have doubled from 40,000 to 85,000 which Longridge attribute to the success of Sport Unlimited in terms of funding and increased opportunities for young people to experience such activities, who then return outside of Sport Unlimited sessions.

Sport Unlimited deliverers have also provided experiences of certain sports or activities during taster sessions, using technology in a controlled and cost effective environment. Northumberland Sport used 'Concept2' electronic rowing machines to provide individual physical activity sessions to SU participants both male and female aged 11–19. During the taster sessions, participants who showed willingness and an aptitude for rowing were then signposted to a rowing club in their area to experience the real thing. Other APAs delivered using such technology have proved useful in a variety of ways in engaging young people with a disability, such as 'dance mats' and 'Wii fit' provided in a safe, fun and controlled environment. For instance, 'Wii Tennis' was delivered by West Yorkshire Sport to demonstrate the sport and encourage young people to develop their confidence and feel able to go out onto the court to try tennis. Another example is 'Wii dance', where movement patterns could be demon-strated, an activity which retained 50 out of 51 young people in West Yorkshire in the term it was delivered. However, Wii has only been used on a limited number of occasions where there is a specific need to engage a certain group of participants in an activity before they transition to the actual activity, which makes up the majority of the delivery.

Through Sport Unlimited, APA deliverers have proved to be proactive in marketing the activities; signposting children to clubs; providing innovative service delivery; rewarding or incentivising participation and consulting before and during the programme to improve the service on offer. Overall, many of the activities have been delivered in an environment which suits the ability levels, activity preferences and personalities of young people because of the volume of activities on offer. The challenge for many APAs, particularly those which have developed at a local level through Sport Unlimited, is whether they can sustain their provision and also maintain parti-cipant interest to allow for young people to continue participating once the Sport Unlimited programme finishes in 2011.

Conclusions

This paper set out to highlight the significance of alternative physical activities in engaging young people in sport and physical activity, alongside the more traditional activities on offer. The paper discussed how the definition of alternative physical activities is rather vague and highlighted how many authors have offered varying definitions of the phrase.

It is evident that generally the term APAs encompasses non traditional sporting activities which often incorporate an element of adventure. The research has highlighted how recent policy interventions acknowledge that young people have varying needs and preferences and that programmes and interventions are taking this into consideration by offering a variety of opportunities to ensure young people engage with such programmes aimed at increasing participation in sport and physical activity. It is also evident that the National Curriculum is playing an increasingly prominent role in the provision of APAs, and that schools are also recognising the importance of APAs which is evidenced by a clear increase in the provision of activities within PE timetables. This is helping to create an opening for young people to further develop their skills, interests and motivation to participate, helping to promote lifelong participation.

The research has categorised the 147 sports recognised by Sport England into the six themes delivered under the National Curriculum guidelines. It revealed that 47% of these sports were classified as alternative activities and 91% of these are part of Sport England's 46 funded sports for the period 2009–2013. This has highlighted the volume of APAs for potential participation under the National Curriculum categories. Furthermore, the paper has reported how Sport England's Sport Unlimited programme has been inspirational in dedicating resources to encourage more semi sporty young people to take part in more sport or physical activity by offering an array of attractive opportunities, with over 100 variations of APAs offered throughout the Sport Unlimited programme alone.

The research highlighted that Active People 3 and Sport Unlimited data suggests (where data was available) that some of the APAs offered in the National Curriculum are more popular with the generation of young people who have been exposed to additional extra curricular opportunities in the last decade. It remains to be seen whether or not the offer of APAs helps to encourage lifelong participation and drive up participation rates generally across the country. However, offering young people something away from the mainstream is important in helping to inspire further participation with the aim of encouraging a physically active nation.

The Comprehensive Spending Review (2010) announced reductions in funding for sport and the structures which have been created in sport development over the last decade. A reduction in budgets on the supply side has the potential to impact on policies designed to shape tastes and preferences for young people, the group where the harnessing of positive attitudes towards active lifestyles begins. Sport Unlimited, as part of the five hour offer, has played an important role in delivering sessions which were previously unavailable, particularly through the current network which facilitates the introduction to a wide range of sports and activities. However, the changing landscape in school sport funding and focus, in particular the increased focus on competition, has implications on the future provision (and growth of) APAs within the school sport setting. It is likely that competition structures will, in most instances, be set up around traditional sports which are within the curriculum. The role of alternative activities in competition structures may, therefore, be limited or reduced. This focus may also impinge upon the participation of those individuals who want to take part in sport but may not want to do so in a competitive environment. Competition is a vital part of sporting provision for young people and should be a significant part of policy; however this should be understood in the wider context that not all young people want to compete but do want to take part in sport in some form.

References

Beal, B. (2001) 'Disqualifying the official: An exploration of social resistance through the subculture of skateboarding', in A. Yiannakis, and M.J. Melnick (eds) *Contemporary issues in sociology of sport*. Champaign Illinois: Human Kinetics.

Bloyce, D. and Smith, A. (2010) *Sport policy and development an introduction*. Oxon: Routledge.

Booth, D. and Thorpe, H. (2007) 'The meaning of Extreme', in'*Berkshire encyclopaedia of extreme sport*. Thorpe Great Barrington. Berkshire: Berkshire Reference Works.

Boyle, L., Jones, G. and Walters, S. (2008) 'Physical activity among adolescents and barriers to delivering PE in Cornwall and Lancashire, UK: A qualitative study of heads of PE'and heads of schools', *BMC Public Health* Vol. 8: pp. 273.

Bullough, S., Hart, G. and Gregory, M. (2011) 'Demand for sport: What young people want', in Jeanes, R. and Magee, J. (eds) *Children, Youth and Leisure*, LSA Publication No. 113. Eastbourne: Leisure Studies Association, pp. 55–80.

Cale, L. and Harris, J. (2006) 'School-based physical activity interventions: effectiveness, trends, issues, implications and recommendations for practice', *Sport Education and Society* Vol. 11, No. 4: pp. 401–420.

Coakley, J. (2004) *Sport in society: Issues and controversies (8th Edition)*. London: McGraw-Hill.

Coakley, J. and Whilte, A. (1992) 'Making decisions: Gender and sport participation among British adolescents', *Sociology of Sport Journal* Vol. 9, No. 1: pp. 20–35.

Coalter, F. (1996) *Trends in Sports Participation*. Position paper prepared for Sports Council: UK.

Department for Children, Schools and Families (2008) *School Sport Survey 2007/2008*. London: Department for Children, Schools and Families.

Department for Culture, Media and Sport / Strategy Unit (2002a) *Game plan: A strategy for delivering Government's sport and physical activity objectives*. London: Strategy Unit.

Department for Culture, Media and Sport (2002b) *Learning through PE and sport; A guide to the physical education, school sport and club links strategy*. London: Department for Culture Media and Sport.

Department for Education (2010) *A new approach for school sports — decentralising power, incentivising competition, trusting teachers*. Press release, 20th December 2010 accessed from http://www.education.gov.uk/inthenews/pressnotices/a0071098/a-new-approach-for-school-sports-decentralising-power-incentivising-competition-trusting-teachers 23rd February, 2011.

Downward, P., Dawson, A. and Dejonghe, T. (2009) *Sports economics: Theory, policy and evidence*. Amsterdam; London: Butterworth-Heinemann.

Evans, J. (1990) 'Defining the subject: The rise and rise of the new PE', *British Journal of Sociology of Education* Vol. 11, No. 2: pp. 155–69.

Evans, J. Penney, D. Bryant, A. and Hennick, M. (1996) 'All things bright and beautiful? PE in primary schools post the 1988 ERA', *Educational Review* Vol. 48, No. 1: pp. 29–40

Grainger-Jones, B. (1999) *Managing leisure*. Oxford: Butterworth Heinemann.

Gratton, C. and Taylor, P. (2000) *Economics of sport and recreation*. London: E and FN SPON.

Green, K. (2002) 'Physical education and the couch potato society', *European Journal of Physical Education* Vol. 7, No. 2: pp. 95–107.

Hellison, D., Cutforth, N., Kallusky, J., Martinek, T., Parker, M. and Stiehl, J. (2000) *Youth development and physical activity: Linking universities and communities*. London: Human Kinetics.

HM Treasury (2010) *Spending Review 2010*. London: HM Treasury.

Honeybourne, J., Hill, M. and Moors, H. (2004) *Advanced PE and sport: Third Edition*. Cheltenham: Nelson Thornes Ltd.

Houlihan, B. (2008) *Sport and society. A student introduction. Second Edition*. London: Sage.

Hylton, K. and Bramham, P. (2007) *Sport development: Policy, process and practice. Second Edition.* London: Routledge.

Keighley, P. W. S. (1993) 'A consideration of the appropriate teaching, learning and assessment strategies in the outdoor adventurous activity element of outdoor education as it relates to the physical education National Curriculum', *British Journal of Physical Education* Vol. 24, No. 1: pp. 18–22.

Kirk, D. (1998) *Schooling bodies: School practice and public discourse 1880–1950.* London: Leicester University Press.

—— (2005) 'Physical'education, youth sport and lifelong participation: The importance of early learning experiences', *European Education Review* Vol. 11, No. 3: pp. 239–255.

Loughborough Partnership (2005) *School sport partnerships: Monitoring and evaluation report 2004.* Loughborough: Institute of Youth Sport, Loughborough University.

—— (2006) *School sport partnerships: Annual monitoring and evaluation report for 2005.* Loughborough: Institute of Youth Sport, Loughborough University.

Love, C. (2007) 'State schools, swimming and physical training', *International Journal of the History of Sport* Vol. 24, No. 5: pp. 654–666.

Mangan, J. A. (2010) 'Athleticism: a case study of the evolution of an educational ideology', *International Journal of the History of Sport* Vol. 27, No. 1: pp. 60–77.

McNamee, M. (2006) *Philosophy, risk and adventure sports.* London: Routledge.

Midol, N. and Broyer, G. (1995) 'Towards an anthropological analysis of new sport cultures: the case of whiz sports in France', *Sociology of Sport Journal* Vol. 12, No. 2: pp. 204–212.

Mintel (2003) *Extreme Sports, Leisure Intelligence.* London: Mintel International Group Ltd.

Mulvihill, C., Rivers, K. and Aggleton, P. (2000) 'Views of young people towards physical activity: Determinants and barriers to involvement', *Health Education* Vol. 100, No. 5: pp. 190–199.

Office for National Statistics (1971–2003) *The General Household Survey.* London: Office for National Statistics.

—— (2010) 'Mid year population estimates 2009. Table 4: England 2009'. Online, last accessed 24th November 2010 from http://www.statistics.gov.uk/statbase/Product.asp?vlnk= 15106

Office for Standards in Education (2003) *The school sport coordinator programme: Evaluation of phases 1 and 2, 2001–2003.* London: Office for Standards in Education (OFSTED).

—— (2004) *The school sport coordinator programme: Evaluation of phases 3 and 4, 2001–2003.* London: Office for Standards in Education (OFSTED).

—— (2005) *The physical education, school sport and club links strategy: The school sport partnership programme. Support for gifted and talented pupils in physical education.* London: Crown (OFSTED).

—— Children's Services and Skills (2009) *Physical education in schools 2005–8*. London: Office for Standards in Education, Children's Services and Skills (OFSTED).

Penney, D. and Evans, J. (1999) *Politics, policy and practice in physical education*. London: E and FN SPON.

Rinehart, R. and Sydnor, S. (2003) *To the extreme: Alternative sports inside and out*. New York: State University of New York Press.

Roberts, K. (1996) 'Young people, schools, sport and government policy', *Sport, Education and Society* Vol. 1, No. 1: pp. 47–57.

—— (1999) *Leisure in contemporary society*. Wallingford: CABI Publications.

Sport England (2002) *Young People and Sport Survey 2002*. London: Sport England.

—— (2008a) Sport Unlimited project outline. Online, last accessed 1st November 2010 from http://www.sportengland.org/support_advice/children_and_young_people/community_and_ club_activities/sport_unlimited.aspx

—— (2008b) *Sport England Strategy 2008–2011*. London: Sport England.

—— and Youth Sport Trust (2009a) *PE and sport strategy for young people: A guide to delivering the five hour offer*. London: Sport England.

—— (2009b) *Active People Survey 3*. London: Sport England.

—— (2010a) *How we recognise sports*. Online, last accessed 15th October 2010 from http://www.sportengland.org/about_us/how_we_recognise_sports/recognised_sports_and_ngbs.aspx

—— (2010b) *Sports market segmentation web tool*. London: Sport England. Online tool, last accessed 18th November, from http://segments.sportengland.org/

Thorpe, H. and Rinehart, R. (2010) 'Alternative sport and affect: Non-representational theory examined', *Sport in Society* Vol. 13, No. 7: pp. 1268–1291.

Tomlinson, A., Ravenscroft, N., Wheaton, B. and Gilchrist, P. (2005) *Lifestyle sports and national sports policy: An agenda for research. Report to Sport England*. London: Sport England.

Wheaton, B. (2010) 'Introducing the consumption and representation of lifestyle sports', *Sport in Society* Vol. 13, No. 7/8: pp. 1057–1081.

—— (2004) *Understanding lifestyle sports. Consumption, identity and difference*. London: Routledge.

Willig, C. (2008) 'A phenomenological investigation of the experience of taking part in extreme sports', *Journal of Health Psychology* Vol. 13, No. 5: pp. 690–702.

Universities and Colleges Application Service (2010) *Courses starting in 2011*. Online, last accessed 22nd November 2010 from http://www.ucas.com/students/coursesearch/2011searcheu/

BOXING, CULTURE AND SOCIETY: DEVELOPING WINNERS THROUGH THE 'SPORT ETHIC'?

Alex Stewart

University of Bedfordshire

The Government vision for sport in Britain deems that participation in and through sport encourages a form of 'salubrious socialisation' to take place resulting in 'better' societies (Green, 2008: p. 130). With the London 2012 Olympic Games in the foreground, the lead documents outlining the social significance of sport in the UK and England — *Game Plan: A strategy for achieving Government's sport and physical activity objectives* (DCMS, 2002) and *Playing to Win: A new era for sport* (DCMS, 2008) — have proclaimed, albeit from arguably divergent 'social intervention' and 'performance and excellence' emphases, sport's intrinsic and extrinsic potential.

The heralding of sport as an inherently positive agent of personal and social change has, of course, not gone unchallenged. As Kidd (1996: p. 84) notes, "... there is no guarantee that the provision of difficult challenges set through sporting competition is in itself educational in a humane, beneficial, or ethical way". Similarly, much scholarly commentary on sport development policy has been skeptical about the "...myths and storylines, which generate and preserve (generally positive) perceptions of sport development on the basis of weak evidence" (Houlihan, 2010: p. 1). Furthermore, as Spaaij (2009) points out, individual and social change as perceived by those affected by it often represents a 'developmental' process that may produce both positive and negative consequences. In regard to the policy context of UK sport delivery, as elsewhere, it is important to acknowledge the power of those advocating the "... supposed moral aura" (Houlihan, 2010: p. 3) of sport's developmental potential, one that has persisted since the nineteenth century, and the extent to which such definitions remain uncritically accepted by policy makers to this

75

day. Equally, it is necessary to acknowledge that somewhat lost within the web of UK sports development policy are the voices and subjectivities of those being 'developed' (Girginov, 2008; Houlihan and Green, 2010). This essay seeks to redress this imbalance by drawing upon ethnographic data collected over a five-year period among amateur and professional boxing-practitioners based in Luton and London, England, as part of my doctorial studies. The methodological imperative of the research was, in part, to investigate the social and cultural significance of amateur and professional boxing as understood from the boxing-practitioners' own worldviews, embodied experiences and symbolic articulations, and the limits and possibilities of their association with boxing henceforth (see Stewart, 2008).

In terms of exploring the developmental potential of boxing in England, the task of this essay is twofold. In the first instance, I offer insight into how amateur boxers and significant others in some way responsible for their welfare make sense of their lived experiences in and through boxing, while grounding their subjective perceptions in the wider academic and policy debate regarding the role of sport/ boxing as a process of personal and social change. In doing so, this essay also addresses the extent to which the 'sport ethic' of boxing acts as a dynamic'and embodied socio-cultural force mediating and (re)producing 'developmental' processes through which the reconstruction of subjectivities and (simultaneously) positive and negative social change may take place. As is shown below, English amateur boxing-practitioners' understandings of the 'sport ethic' are complex, incorporating the subtle interweaving of dominant political visions regarding the role of sport as an agent for positive personal and social change, with the interplay between residual and emergent cultural resources through which they construct experience and identity. The socio-historical processes through which 'boxing', as an amateur *and* professional cultural phenomenon, structure the lived experiences of boxers in the present moment is discussed next.

Boxing and culture through history

Boxing is one of the oldest and enduringly most popular mainstream sports in Britain (and overseas) followed by thousands sitting ringside and millions by way of televised broadcast (Boyle and Haynes 2009; Sugden, 1996). Boxing also entices the active engagement of thousands of boys and men, and increasingly girls and women, in most cities and towns in England — whether as keep-fit recreation or as a more serious (i.e. competitive) athletic pursuit (Sport England, 2009). As a social practice boxing in England (and overseas) has historically been organized into two distinctive codes each with its own long established traditions and conventions — amateur and professional boxing (Shipley, 1989).

Since its inception in 1880, the Amateur Boxing Association of England (ABAE) has governed its own schedule of competition for amateur boxing-practitioners affiliated to over eight-hundred amateur boxing clubs situated in most cities and towns in England (McNab, 2001). The professional code of boxing in England, on the other hand, is organized under the aegis of the British Boxing Board of Control (BBBC) and is practised within a somewhat subterranean network of gymnasiums located in the inner cities and surrounding conurbations of Britain's largest post-industrial metropolises (Sipley 1989). The historical split between the amateur and professional codes can be more succinctly understood as a consequence of the wider processes of social transformation and struggle taking place during the social stratification of industrial Britain from the nineteenth century onwards. As such, both codes adopted distinctive ideological visions regarding the meanings in and values inherent through sporting competition.

The amateur code of boxing derives its sense of place and culture from the 'not-for-money' ideology of sporting amateurism, born of the Victorian public school system, subsequently diffused to the masses via the institutionalisation of popular sporting pastimes, including boxing (Hargreaves, 1986). The provision of amateur boxing 'for all' has been in part attributed to an initiative of Muscular Christian reform propagated to the 'lower orders' via the church and other social agencies (Holt, 1989; Mangan, 1981). In this guise, amateur boxing was conceived as a tool promoting lessons in health, education and morality to the working classes. As Holt (1989) in particular has noted, boxing was readily endorsed as a moral antidote to perceived social problems among the 'roughs' in society, particularly those massed in the cityscapes of industrialised Britain. Of course, such initiatives also served the needs of industrial owners, who saw the function of sport as an opportunity to cultivate a more disciplined, cohesive and productive workforce. Amateur boxing was believed to be particularly useful in this regard as it served purpose for disciplining a potentially unruly workforce via a suitably regulated yet appropriately 'rough' sporting outlet (Shipley, 1989; Sugden 1996). A clear illustration of the residual ideological power defining the value of amateur boxing for both boxer and society today is evidenced in Saintsbury's publication '*In Praise of Boxing — an exposition of a great sport*' (1999)[1]. Repeatedly making reference to boxing as the 'Noble

Art of Self–Defence', Sainstsbury insists that boxing instills in many young men from underprivileged backgrounds a spirit of discipline through which they develop respect for self and others that also often deters a life of crime. Moreover, 'the sportsmanship of the ring' is nurtured as a consequence of the altruistic army of volunteers who spend much of their free time coaching and administering the sport they love. Hence, the particular cultural affinity for boxing held by those eking out a living in the poorer sectors of society has an invaluable role to play in the development of the individual, the social fabric of their immediate community and the wider society.

In sharp contrast to the 'Sport for All' amateur(ism) code, professional boxing in England emerged from the outlawed and hugely popular practice of pugilism (Brailsford, 1988). Retaining affinity with their pugilistic ancestors' interest in fighting for a monetary prize, professional boxing in England developed under the governance of the National Sporting Club, an influential and affluent social clique of late nineteenth century London (Holt, 1989). The opportunity extended to professional boxers, nearly all of whom hailed from working-class backgrounds and long steeped in the traditions of pugilism, to profit from a field of autonomous and skilled enterprise contemptuous of the pretensions of 'Shamateurism'[2] (Sewart, 1985) held powerful symbolic resonance for those able or willing enough to take their chances in the ring. Thus, although the amateur and professional codes emerged in close social approximation, on an organizational, ideological and symbolic level professional boxing was conceived as being a rather elitist "... sub-culture within a culture" (Shipley, 1989: p. 90). Today, despite the virtual extinction of a 'pure' amateur ideal associated with the global stage of high performance sport (Allison, 2001), the organisational and spatial separation demarcating amateur boxing from its professional cousin largely remains intact (McNab, 2001). That said, however, as for previous generations the cultural production of professional boxing continues to attract the interest of millions in the UK and beyond (Boyle and Haynes, 2009; Sugden 1996).

Following on from this brief discussion of the organizational and social structures serving to demarcate yet culturally enmesh amateur and professional boxing in England, it is important to explore the ways contemporary amateur boxing-practitioners understand and seek empowerment through boxing. In the following section I incorporate ethnographic narrative to explore one such instance of cultural production through which a group of influential English amateur boxing-practitioners created 'stories' (Coakley and Pike, 2009) of and collectively ascribed meaning to the 'sport ethic' of boxing.

For love of 'The Game'

It is mid-2006 and I'm sitting amongst a nearly all-male group of fifty or so newly appointed 'Development Commissioners' in the bar of the Union Jack Club — a hotel in central London — after just having attended the launch of the Amateur Boxing Association of England's 'Whole Sport Plan'[3]. While the Commissioners enthusiastically discussed the future of their beloved sport and its potential for beneficially socialising thousands of boys and men — and increasingly girls and women — as 'no other sport can', Amir Khan's latest professional contest was aired 'live' by Sky sports. The still boyish looking Athens Olympian and now hot prospect of the professional boxing circuit made his way to the ring flanked by an entourage holding Pakistani and Union Jack flags, with his medal-winning Athens contests shown on a large screen as he entered center stage. The audience packed into the arena either vociferously chanted support for the Olympic hero or, it seemed in equal measure, booed his arrival to the ring. With the MC's introduction of both boxers stirring the vocal exchanges between the fans into fever pitch, the ring emptied and a lull ensued as the two boxers stood alone and readied themselves for battle. In just a few minutes Khan stood over his dazed and bleeding adversary to the vociferous approval of his supporters. While 'the opponent' bowed through the ring ropes all but unnoticed by the majority of those sitting ringside, dozens of journalists crowded around the ring apron to record the rather considered celebrations of this athletically gifted and personable youngster. Before the curtain was drawn on the night's sporting theatre, Khan indulged the Sky-sports interviewer by confidently declaring to the millions at home or in bars similar to this one that he planned to conquer the world of professional boxing, while earning a fortune and making Britain proud at the same time. Meanwhile in the Union Jack Club bar, the Commissioners casually took stock as this latest snippet of boxing history unfolded, intermittently sharing opinions and anecdotes concerning Khan's and a host of other talented ex-amateur boxers' chances of 'making it in the pro game'. While indulging my own thoughts I noticed that barely an eyebrow was raised at the brutal outcome of the contest or, in fact, the well-being of 'the opponent'. Nonetheless, as is discussed below, it is the silence emanating from such a seemingly innocuous instance of popular cultural entertainment that, in many ways, reveals the rather 'hidden' social and cultural processes through which boxing-practitioners attach developmental possibilities to the role of boxing in their lives.

The 'sport reflex-ethic'

A new level of critical sociological analysis of boxing has generated valuable insights regarding the processes that consciously and unconsciously may inform boxing-practitioners' cultural attachments to the 'sport ethic' of boxing. In particular, insightful arguments regarding connections between "two of the great forces of 20th century popular culture" (Boyle and Haynes: 2009 p. 3) — the media and sport — and the ways in which individual subjectivities and collective identities are constructed through media representations of boxing more generally (Delgado, 2005; Woodward, 2008) and Amir Khan in particular (Burdsey, 2007; Boyle and Haynes, 2009) have been made. Woodward (2008) discusses in much detail how various sporting media construct 'heroic' and 'spectacular' boxing narratives, packaged for the consumption of a (predominantly) male audience. In this way, mytho-heroic cultural representations permeate the consciousness of boxing-practitioners in synthesis with their embodied gymnasium experiences and rather more routine social interactions and practices framing their everyday experiences. Correspondingly, for Woodward, an explanation for the enduring appeal of boxing, a dangerous and violent anomaly when contrasted to other more 'civilized' activities, is that "... boxing carries the promise of risk" (2008: p. 2). Thus, those who are drawn to the sport of boxing, either as practitioners or fans, have been attracted by conscious/unconscious processes of identification through which they strive to establish a more secure sense of 'traditional' and hegemonic masculinity in a rapidly transforming, and thus increasingly uncertain and politicized, socio-cultural landscape. The 'sport ethic' of boxing is thus a social and cultural force enmeshing both "fantasy and reality" (Woodward, 2008: p. 4).

Following the literature it can be inferred that the Development Commissioners' individual and collective identification with Khan's athletic prowess, as an Olympic medalist, enmeshed ideological notions of the 'sport ethic' of boxing as morally virtuous, particularly for'working-class boys and men. It may also be suggested, however, that the same instance of cultural production fused processes of conscious/unconscious identification with the razzmatazz media portrayal of Khan's unequivocal masculine dominance as he proceeded to knock unconscious the (for the time being) rather insignificant, and thus 'identity-neutral', figure of the 'opponent'. Khan's opponent remained identity-neutral in this context because, as Maguire (2009) observes, elite sport offers a dramatic and public representation of who we are and/or who we would like to be. Correspondingly, our infatuation with the 'winners' of sport and the stories told and accolades heaped upon them (or not, as is inevitable in sporting competition), are in essence symbolic metaphors of our own cultural identifications, aspirations and biases. Thus, as Delgado (2005), Burdsey (2007) and Boyle and Haynes (2009) argue, it is imperative to acknowledge that processes of identification through the cultural production of boxing are complex and often contradictory as they intersect practices, relations and discourses that inevitably entail boundary marking around class, ethnicity, race and gender. From this perspective it is important to acknowledge that the 'sport ethic' of boxing acts as an embodied and dynamic social and cultural force through which not only subjective struggle but also'group identity politics take place. Thus, as a socio-cultural phenomenon, boxing exhibits the potential to be an agent for both social cohesion and social separation. The following sections of this essay draw upon the voices of boxing-practitioners and my own ethnographic findings to demonstrate how the social and cultural processes articulated above mediated and reproduced (simultaneously) positive and negative developmental outcomes among one particular cohort of amateur boxing practitioners — 'The Gym'.

Amateur boxing for 'boy and club'

Virtually without exception, the boxing-practitioners encountered during the research were adamant that amateur boxing served as a disciplining regime, inculcating youthful social-actors against the ever present risks defining their sense of place in society. During a coaching seminar hosted by the Amateur Boxing Association of England, 'Mickey', a coach of an amateur boxing club based in the Home Counties, revealed deeply felt convictions of the social benefits engineered through amateur boxing:

"There's so much good that can come out of boxing...the old saying about getting kids off the streets and keeping them from mixing with the rubbish that's going on these days...the drugs and the guns and this sort of thing... I think if you go in the large inner cities its only too true, it does an awful lot for them. It gives them something to do, somewhere to be at, an outlet to look forward to that's positive for them...if nothing else purely as a means to channel their aggression in the gym...in a way that is safe and they enjoy it. They develop positive attributes as opposed to negative ones. Boxing is always under control — it is at my place anyway. I coach boxing as sports-science or an art, if you like. That's the way I like them to develop as boxers and they're trained up like that. It does them a world of good. It's like they're in the army for a stint really. It teaches them discipline, self-respect and above all respect for others and that's what it's all about. Kids are kids and you get all types, all kinds of personalities...it's always there... aggression and all that macho in-your-face stuff. You'll never take it away...but on the whole they're good kids. As long as they're behaving, learning and developing their skills in the ring in a controlled way then it's of great benefit to them. I'd rather have my boy in the gym than on the streets, in the pubs or wherever, out of control gone crazy."

The functional value of boxing as a cathartic measure preventing the ills of inner-city moral meltdown is, in this case, infused with axioms of army discipline, scientific exactitude and the expressive aestheticism of sport-replicating-art. The sentiments of assistant coach 'Mickey' were often endorsed by many boxers. Here 'Mo' elaborates when being asked if he thought boxing had changed him in any way:

"As it happens yeah a lot ... if I hadn't been boxing I think I would have been out on the streets hanging around with a bad crowd, you know? I mean perhaps taking drugs ... stealing ... you know ... messing around basically. [Really?] Yeah, I think so because you look around and there's not much you know ... round where I live there's bad influences everywhere, and you take a look at a lot of the Asians out there ... they are all at it ... so I think boxing has taught me a lot ... hmm ... discipline.
[Q] — "You really think you would have got into drugs?"
"You never know ... [contemplative] ... I think what boxing has done is kept me off the streets ... definitely ... because when you think about it, every time you go to the gym it keeps your mind clean as it's thinking about training."

In the words of 'Mo' and many other amateur boxers who were quick to express likewise sentiments, value or profit from their participation in amateur boxing was expressed in terms of the function of sport as a positive socialising agent, particularly for those in some way prone to the risks of street violence, drug abuse and crime. From this standpoint, the 'sport ethic' of amateur boxing encourages a belief in the value of 'honest' — i.e. disciplined and respectful — behaviour, a health-conscious lifestyle and an expressive sensibility through which to achieve a physically virile brand of 'worthy' self-actualisation. In many ways my ethnographic findings endorsed such functionalist logic, in as much as throughout the sustained period of data collection the boxing-practitioners observed adopted remarkably egalitarian codes of conduct as members of a socially diverse (in terms of ethnicity, 'race', religion, age and to a lesser extent gender) collective of practitioners. The 'structure of feeling' (Williams, 1961) through which 'The Gym' members constructed 'respectful' value orientations can be more fully understood as a consequence of the appeal of boxing to be emotionally empowering and socially validating on a cultural level grounded in embodied experience and steeped in symbolism.

Feeling 'it'

A striking feature of the sociability enacted among Gym-practitioners during nightly training sessions was the support offered by a core of Dads in attendance on a regular basis. Volunteering a helping hand with the rudiments of gymnasium maintenance and on occasions contributing financially towards the purchase of equipment for the use of 'all the boys', they considered their input an integral feature of 'The Gym' community. 'Trevor' elaborates on his attendance during most Gym training sessions in accompaniment of his fourteen year-old son 'Ben':

> "I come here to support Ben obviously but I'm interested in all the boys really. If I'm honest all I probably would be doing at home right now is be fast asleep in front of the box. You know how it is ... work all day, get home, switch the television on, have a bite to eat and that's it, into the 'morrow ... Besides Jan [his wife] is working shifts at the airport anyway, so I just sit there on my lonesome so I don't mind getting out. And you know'... Ben is my youngest and the other two, who are a fair bit older, I missed a lot when they were doing their thing. It was just a time I was doing lots of hours and I didn't ... well I couldn't ... spend as much time as I would have liked with them, seeing them grow-up and supporting them more I guess ... So that's another reason I like coming here to spend time with him and support him in what he loves to do." (Fieldnotes, 2005)

'Richie', in accompaniment of his seventeen year-old son 'Dean', was also in attendance on most training nights. In equally earnest vocabulary he expanded upon the recreational motive for his son's and his own approach to boxing, in preference to the array of choices available for a young man on the brink of adulthood:

"The reason I'm here is pure and simple, Deano enjoys it ... that's it. I'm not the type to push it ... you know what I mean Alex? He just likes to come down here, keep fit, train with the lads and he's enjoying competing. You know, he's at an age now ... well he's getting his own mind and well ... [laughs] ... if I tell him one thing or the other it's just not happening! Its been difficult the last year mind 'cause he is flat out working so he's been a bit tired ... but next year he's at college doing a course so he's all for getting into it proper like ... I mean he's out on the town with his mates now he's got some spend'... early manhood and all that ... he likes a game of football also ... but ... he's a steady lad you know what I mean? He goes out with his mates but also likes his boxing ... he likes doing his own thing away from the boys I guess and as long as he wants to ... [emphasising] ... he's enjoying what he's doing, what he's accomplishing and that makes me happy." (Fieldnotes, 2005)

Following the emotional support Dads often attached to their son's motivations to pursue boxing, the boxers interviewed in this study were near unanimous in paying homage to the 'art of boxing' as a highly skilled athletic practice. When asked why they were motivated to dedicate much of their free time to the pursuit of such a physically demanding and potentially risky sport as boxing, they often constructed responses through adopting the discourses from ABAE coaching manuals: physical conditioning drills adapted specifically for the duration of amateur contests; the technical intricacies of balance, timing and hand-eye co-ordination; pivotal leverage; defensive tactics; ring control and the like. Moreover, as well as emphasising their creative agency in striving to master the rudiments of boxing technique, the respondents readily endorsed the sensuous appeal and emotionally captivating 'buzz' generated through the combative element of boxing competition. In turn, it was understood that to improve one's standing as a 'real' (i.e. competitive) boxer it was necessary to be diligent in pursuing a high level physical fitness in order to refine boxing-technique by way of developing bio-mechanical dexterity, mental focus and, more crucially, emotional control. The daily regimens of boxing training thus enabled practitioners to actualise a level of psycho-somatic awareness, expressivity and self-control perhaps unavailable in other social arenas available to them. Furthermore, the findings revealed that if boxing experientially is perhaps the prototypical expression of athletic individualism, it is nonetheless wholly contingent on a hierarchical 'interaction order' (Goffman, 1967), engineering conformity towards a disciplinarian work ethic and respectful behaviour as the norm. In fact, over the five-year period of data collection, no incident of individual or collective resistance by the youthful boxers towards the disciplinarian regime of the 'sport ethic' exerted by Coaches and Dads took place (at least publicly).

Under closer scrutiny, however, the often-voiced claim of disciplinarian, philanthropic and communitarian development as the defining purpose of the 'sport ethic' of amateur boxing, lapsed into ideological discourse not wholly compatible with the values and behaviours enacted among 'The Gym' members.'More poignantly, over the duration of fieldwork it became increasingly evident that a Weberian 'gain spirit' (Weber, 2001), punctuated by dubiety and tension, pervaded the social interactions of The Gym's cohort of boxing-practitioners[4]. It is at this juncture that it is possible to be critical of the functionalist logic through which the 'sport ethic' of amateur boxing is envisaged as being a positive socialising agent for both the boxer and the society s/he lives in.

Winning through the 'sport ethic'?

As never before in accordance to Government policy, the most comprehensive program of funding for the development of amateur boxers capable of medal successes prior to the imminent London 2012 Olympic Games is in place. Nonetheless, the policy vision for doing so seamlessly conflates 'Prolympic' (Donnelly, 1996) — the confluence of Olympic and Professional — standards of athletic excellence with sporting participation for all. It can be deduced, therefore, that if the contemporary policy agenda serves to motivate boxing-practitioners to aspire 'upwards' by continually striving to surpass the constraints of their immediate life-circumstances then, by definition, this is a laudable sentiment. This frame of logic, however, is troubling as it may just as well encompass debates critical of the commercial and human exploitation associated with professional boxing (Sugden, 1996; Wacquant, 2004), as well as those identifying the decline of sporting ideals enshrining ethics of selfless altruism due to the rise of sporting commodification across the globe (Donnelly, 1996; Ingham, 2004; Horne, 2006; Walsh and Giulianotti, 2007).

As my discussion has indicated, boxing-practitioners' understandings of development are contextually grounded not merely in wider sports policy but also in the residual and emergent traditions through which 'boxing' — both in its amateur and professional guise — has been practised for many centuries. Accordingly, it was clearly the case that significant others responsible for amateur boxer's development normatively expressed deeply felt philanthropic and nurturing sentiments that, indeed, guided their values and practices. Nonetheless, under a veneer of altruism, fellowship and collective passion for the character-reforming qualities inherent to the 'sport ethic' of amateur boxing, it was also the case that inter-personal and group power struggles ensued among boxing-practitioners, on many levels. A dominant theme that emerged from this research was the antipathy, at times hostility, displayed by 'The Gym' practitioners towards the ABAE officials volunteering their free time and effort ostensibly for the boxing-practitioners' benefit. Much as Hoggart (1957) first chronicled the typical resentment working-class spectators held against the referees at rugby league fixtures during the 1950s, it can be inferred that the ABAE officials' administration of 'the rule book', in a bid to ensure equitable competition through fair-play, was perceived by many boxing-practitioners as symbolic of the authoritarian regime defining the workplace and other aspects of their social identities (Hughson *et al.*, 2005).

Nonetheless, far from being merely symbolic acts of resistance through which a collective identity could be claimed in the manner of 'us' and 'them', the manner of resistance I observed throughout the period of my research increasingly took on a rather atomized, vitriolic and, many a time, aggressive character. It was not unusual for large contingents of fans supporting individual boxers to disturb the balance between rule-bound civility and outright hostility in and out of the ring, particularly during prestigious tournaments. On one occasion as the crowd chanted, 'GET INTO HIM ... GO ON KNOCK 'IM OUT!', I wondered at the likely consequences if notions of formality to the proceedings were removed. On another occasion — during the prelim stages of a Schools Championships competition — they were, when a disgruntled referee, infuriated by the abuse he received from a group of fans following the disqualification of 'our boy', simply left the building. The absence of a recognisable authority figure to regulate the contest, however, left a strangely muted crowd staring at the empty ring while wondering how to occupy their time, and the boxing fraternity busy scrutinising, blaming and shaking their heads in disbelief — "all gloved up and nowhere to go", as one wag in the audience quipped. On half a dozen other occasions, however, violence between groups of fans erupted inside and outside of the arena.

The suggestion I make is that fuelling the rather aggressive ambience of dozens of tournaments I attended during the period of data collection is that the policy rhetoric of 'liberal individualism' (Jarvie, 2006) becomes increasingly subsumed within the moral and symbolic compass through which amateur boxing-practitioners construct identity and lived experience. As ethnographers John Sugden (1996) and Loic Wacquant (2004) have observed, the folksy aphorism often voiced by boxers that 'boxing is in the blood' is useful in comprehending the ways the 'sport ethic' of boxing culturally 'inhabited' them and thus gave meaning to their identities, aspirations and experiences as men. The social significance of the 'sport ethic' of amateur boxing can, as such, be understood as a psycho-social force through which men have sought subjective and social empowerment through the timeless eulogy of sporting grit, courage, talent, heart and determination for many generations. In the current moment, however, along with the erosion of 'traditional' social and ideological structures through which boxing had been grounded in community experience, and as such steeped in somewhat more localised and homogeneous cultural codes and conventions (Winlow and Hall, 2006), the metaphoric dimensions linking boxing to 'hegemonic masculinity' (Connell, 1996) are culturally "... retrieved, circulated and reinforced in the media coverage of boxing" (Boyle and Haynes, 2009: p. 139). I suggest, therefore, that amateur boxing-practitioners' values and aspirations are in the present era increasingly premised on identification with 'Prolympic' athletic excellence and/or, far more readily, the 'heroic' and hyper-masculine narratives engineered by the gatekeepers of the professional code of boxing. Furthermore, it can be deduced that the residual amateur 'sport ethic' premised on philanthropic altruism 'for boy and club' increasingly amounts to a 'filtering-mechanism' demarcating, experientially but more importantly symbolically, the performances of 'elite' (Prolympic and professional) boxers from 'the rest'.

If the contemporary era of cultural production increasingly promotes the winning mentality 'for all', then 'losing' and being defined as 'a loser', in or out of the ring, is for many inconceivable or intolerable. Moreover, a readily accessible and increasingly (self)aggrandized symbolic capital is gleaned from the 'spectacular' cultural production of professional boxing. Accordingly, if the developmental potential of the 'sport ethic' of boxing is, to a large extent, to be gained from socially and symbolically anchored validation and admiration for 'pure endeavour', 'skill acquisition', 'fair play' and so on, and consensus that inevitable setbacks are entailed, then the contemporary policy visions through which 'winners' and"losers' are culturally esteemed need careful consideration. The findings of this study suggest that the 'sport ethic' of amateur boxing was understood and acted upon by many boxing-practitioners in the context of broader and declining relationships between community, tradition and identity construction (Layder, 1994). Thus, developmental outcomes through amateur boxing, for both boxer and society, increasingly have the unintended potential to be morally and socially impotent.

Notes

[1] This publication was presented to Parliament in defence of amateur boxing against anti-boxing elements in society, most notably the British Medical Association (see BMA 1996).

[2] 'Shamateurism' is defined by Sewart (1985: p. 78) as "... hypocrisy, violations of antitrust, involuntary servitude, fraud, unenforceable contract, unfair competition, restraint of trade laws, and generally as a code that arbitrarily enforces rules contrary to human rights".

[3] In 2006–7 I served as a Development Commissioner for the Amateur Boxing Association of England

[4] I have to acknowledge my own gain motive either as an athlete and/or researcher was pervasive throughout the period of analysis. As the research process unfolded it became increasingly difficult for me to reconcile what I considered to be inexcusable acts of self-interest from those bearing responsibility for the spirit in which amateur boxing was/ should be practised. I no longer coach at the Gym and hereby lay bare my subjective gaze in the hope that the scope of critical judgment offered (tinged with authorial 'gain motive') is, if nothing else, made transparent to the reader.

References

Burdsey, D. (2007) 'Role with the punches: The construction and representation of Amir Khan as a role model in multiethnic Britain', *Sociological Review* Vol. 55, No. 3: pp. 611–31.

Coakley, J. and Pike, E. (2009) *Sports in society: Issues and controversies.* New York: McGraw-Hill.

Connell, R. (1996) *Masculinities.* Berkeley: University of California Press.

DCMS (Department of Media Culture and Sport) (2002) *Game plan: A strategy for delivering government's sport and physical activity objectives.* London: DCMS.

——— (2008) *Playing to win: A new era for sport. London:* DCMS.

Delgado, F. (2005) 'Golden but not brown: Oscar De La Hoya and the complications of culture, manhood and boxing', *International Journal of the History of Sport* Vol. 22, No. 2: pp. 196–211.

Donnelly, P. (1996) 'Prolympism: Sport monoculture as crisis and opportunity', *Quest* Vol. 48, No. 1: pp. 25–42.

Goffman, E. (1967) *Interaction ritual: Essays on face-to-face interaction.* Oxford: Aldine.

Green, B. C. (2008) 'Sport as an agent for social and personal change', in Girginov, V. (ed) *Management of sport development.* Oxford: Elsevier.

Hargreaves, J. (1986) *Sport, power and culture.* Cambridge: Polity/ Blackwell Publishers.

Hoggart, R. (1957) *The uses of literacy.* London: Chatto and Windus.

Holt, R. (1989) *Sport and the British: A modern history.* Oxford: Clarendon Press.

Horne, J. (2006) *Sport in consumer society*. Basingstoke: Palgrave Macmillan.

Houlihan, B. (2010) 'Introduction', in Houlihan, B. and Green, M. (eds) *Routledge handbook of sports development*. London: Routledge.

Houlihan, B. and Green, M. (eds) (2010) *Routledge handbook of sports development*. London: Routledge.

Hughson, J., Inglis, D. and Free, M. (2005) *The uses of sport: A critical study*. London: Routledge.

Ingham, A. (2004) 'Sportification process: Marx, Weber, Durkheim and Freud', in Giulianotti, R. (ed) *Sport and modern social theorists*. Basingstoke: Palgrave.

Jarvie, G. (2006) *Sport, culture and society: An introduction*. London: Routledge.

Kidd, B. (1996) 'Taking the rhetoric seriously: Proposals for Olympic education', *Quest* Vol. 48, No. 1: pp. 82–92.

Maguire, J. (2009) 'The social construction and impact of champions', *Sport in Society* Vol. 12, No. 9 (November).

Mangan, J. A. (1981) *Athleticism in the Victorian and Edwardian public school*. London: Falmer.

McNab, T. (2001) *Amateur Boxing Association of England: A Report*. London: Sport England.

Saintsbury, G. (1999) *In praise of boxing: An exposition of a great sport*. London: Londsdale Publications.

Sewart J (1985) 'The meaning of amateurism', *Sociology of Sport Journal* Vol. 2, No. 1: pp. 77–86.

Shipley, S. (1989) 'Boxing', in Mason, T. (ed) *Sport in Britain: A social history*. Cambridge: Cambridge University Press.

Spaaij, R. (2009) 'The social impact of sport: Diversities, complexities and contexts', *Sport in Society* Vol. 12, No. 9: November.

Sport England (2009) *Active People Survey (APS) results for Boxing*, Sport England (December).

Stewart, A. (2008) *From the boxer's point of view: A study of cultural production and athletic development among amateur and professional boxers in England*, Unpublished doctoral dissertation, University of Luton.

Sugden, J. (1996) *Boxing and society: An international analysis*. Manchester: Manchester University Press.

Wacquant, L. (2004) *Body and soul: Notebooks of an apprentice boxer*. Oxford: Oxford University Press.

Walsh, A. and Giulianotti, V. (2007) *Ethics, money and sport*. London: Routledge.

Weber, M. (2001) (c1930) *The Protestant ethic and the spirit of capitalism*. London: Routledge.

Williams, R. (1961) *The long revolution*. London: Chatto and Windus.

Winlow, S. and Hall, S. (2006) *Violent night: Urban leisure and contemporary culture*. Oxford: Berg.

Woodward, K. (2008) *Boxing, masculinity and identity*. London: Routledge.

SPORT AND THE CITY: SUB-STATE DIPLOMACY AND THE OLYMPIC BID

Aaron Beacom

University College Plymouth St Mark & St John

Introduction

The city is enshrined in International Olympic Committee (IOC) proto-col as the focal point of the bidding process for the Olympic Games. Yet it is acknowledged that no bid can succeed without the support of the state within which the bidding city is located. This dynamic reflects a deeper tension concerning the role of the city as a political entity in international politics, and was brought into sharp relief in 2005, as three European cities (Paris, Madrid and London) entered the final stage of the bidding process for the 2012 Olympic Games. Martins (2004) contends that the bidding process is integral to the strategy of cities, not just to develop their infrastructure and economy, but also to strengthen their geo-political influence as discreet regional and international entities. European supranational (EU) and intergovern-mental (COE) policy making in areas such as subsidiarity, regional development and municipal authority competencies would appear to support this process.

Such arguments have limitations when considered in the context of the pivotal role of the state in the bidding process for the Olympic Games. This chapter explores new conceptions of diplomacy in rela-tion to the Olympic Movement. It introduces the idea of municipal authorities and other sub-state entities as stakeholders in the Olym-pic bid. These stakeholders have the capacity to pursue their own interests in the bidding process, through forms of diplomatic dis-course previously associated with states and agencies acting on behalf of states. Such activity does not necessarily bring sub-state entities into conflict with the more traditional forms of state diplomacy linked to the Olympic Movement. All stakeholders have a shared interest in securing a successful outcome to the Games and their diplomatic engagement is part of a global network of relationships and lobbying activities. The chapter engages with recent scholarly work in the area of diplomacy and foreign policy and suggests that an appreciation of so-called multi-stakeholder negotiation can provide insights into this dynamic.

Evolving perspectives on diplomacy

The elusive nature of diplomacy creates difficulty for commentators attempting to produce a single, all encompassing definition of the term. Diplomacy narrowly defined is concerned with the protocols and processes by which states "secure the objectives of their foreign policies without resort to force, propaganda or law" (Berridge, 2005: p. 1). Beyond the pursuit of state interests there is a sense that diplomacy is concerned with the wider management of inter-state relations (Ruggie, 2005). The parameters of diplomacy are however increasingly contested as commentators offer different views regarding the role of the state in shaping the terms of reference for diplomatic discourse. On the one hand are those who continue to adopt a relatively narrow definition of diplomacy as essentially statecraft (Watson, 1982). Others focus on the state as the key, though perhaps not the only, actor. Barston (2006) for example, while acknowledging the increasing range of non-state actors who are involved in diplomatic discourse, presents modern forms of diplomacy as evolving through dialogue between states. There is indeed evidence to support the argument that, notwithstanding change in the global environment, diplomatic discourse continues to be shaped by the trappings of state-state relations. Sharp (1999) for example, argues that the increasing number of states emerging from the fragmentation of the Soviet Union and former Yugoslavia has, if anything, enhanced the role of traditional state diplomacy as newly emerging states seek diplomatic recognition through the traditional channels of establishing Embassies and resident diplomats.

A number of writers consider diplomacy as referring to a process of negotiation between collectives that transcends time and space and therefore is not limited to work within a system of sovereign states (Hocking, 2006). Sharp (1999: p. 49) considers the transcendent quality of diplomacy and notes how organizations take on the trappings of diplomacy not because they wish to copy 'state diplomacy' but because there is something 'innate' about diplomatic method that lifts it beyond time and place. In this sense diplomatic method can be said to exist as an identifiable set of mediating and negotiating practices emerging before the modern state system evolved and continuing to exist as the nature of states is transformed and a range of other actors engage in the international system. This latter point is particularly significant since it underpins arguments relating to diplomacy in which terminal authority in the international system does not necessarily lie with the state and where there are a number of levels of authority including municipal and regional bodies, supranational organizations such as the European Union and international organizations such as the United Nations (Sharp, 2009)

Commentary on contemporary diplomatic discourse tends to focus on the exponential growth in the range of agents of diplomacy and how these agents interact (Langhorne, 2005). This should be considered against the backdrop of the wide body of literature dealing variously with the fragmentary nature of modern international society, the increasing number of actors actively engaged in policy processes at sub-national, national and international level and the trend toward interdependence that is a key feature of so-called 'globalization' (Hocking, 2006, Baylis and Smith, 2005, Sharp, 2009). Reinecke (1998) for example, in discussing the impact of globalization on international development, drew attention to the widely held perception among policy makers that globalization has weakened governments. Further, he pointed to the weight of academic research that suggested the significance of states relative to that of:

> other social organizations, such as multinational enterprises, non-governmental organizations and international organizations has been declining as a result of interdependence and globalization, leading to considerable tension between state and non-state actors. (Reinecke 1998: p. 52)

It is against this backdrop that the development of so-called multi-stakeholder diplomacy (Hocking, 2006) should be considered.

Hocking (2006), focusing on the changing culture of diplomacy in the new global environment, suggests that a different perspective is required in order to understand the nature of contemporary diplomatic discourse. He comments on the idea of diplomacy becoming an activity concerned with the creation of networks embracing a range of state and non-state actors focusing on the "management of issues demanding the application of recourses in which no single participant possesses a monopoly" (Hocking, 2006: p. 14). This process has attracted different labels from a range of commentators, in particular multi-stakeholder diplomacy and multi-layered diplomacy. Writers have focused on the increasing complexity of policy processes and the resultant requirement for collaboration. This draws a greater number of actors into the diplomatic process, for example, organizations with specialist knowledge and skills base, across the public, commercial and third sectors. In addition, national governments faced with the complexities of an increasing range of environmental challenges, including global warming, are unable to respond effectively on a national basis and are required to engage with a range of organizations and agencies in negotiating appropriate responses (Betsill and Corell, 2008). Hocking (2006) argues that this fundamentally changes the nature of diplomacy, moving it from being an exclusive process to a more inclusive process resulting from the imperative to work with other actors. He refers to the value of each stakeholder based on their right to be heard resulting from their unique perspective and expertise. In particular, the diplomatic process becomes dependent on 'tri-sectoral' interactions between non-governmental organizations (NGOs), business and government. He stresses that multi-stakeholder diplomacy does not necessarily result in a diminished role for the professional diplomat. Rather that it changes the focus of the professional diplomat from developing relationships and engaging directly in negotiation, toward facilitating contacts between stakeholders. As a 'boundary spanner' (Hocking, 2006) the diplomat is required to manage relations between increasing numbers of actors involved in negotiation processes. In such a situation, the boundaries between these actors become fluid (for example between the public and private spheres) and there is, if anything, an increased need for skilful mediators.[1]

The argument concerning the ongoing diffusion of power and authority in the international arena tends to revolve around the idea that the authority of the state is being gradually undermined, in part as a result of the process of globalization (Pluijm, 2007, Sharp, 2009). This contention is linked to the emergence of new actors in the diplomatic frame. It is in this context that the argument of promoting the city as an actor in international diplomacy, including the soft diplomacy of lobbying to secure international events, gains credence. The authority and influence of the city in regional and international politics has a long history, from the influence of Greek city states shaping regional relations during the ascendancy of ancient Greek civilization to the role of Italian city states during the Renaissance period (Pluijm, 2007). European and North American cities have, particularly during the nineteenth and twentieth centuries, been asserting themselves as hubs for industrialization, trade and technological advancement. The convergence of a number of wider geo-political trends from the 1980s onwards, namely globalization, the acceleration of European integration and the decentralization process, has, argues Martins (2004), weakened the state and enhanced the potential for other actors to engage in the international arena. Martins (2004) identifies the efforts of European institutions, in particular the Council of Europe, in attempting to create the institutional and legislative framework within which cities could develop as entities distinct from states. One example of this was the 1985 treaty: the European Charter of Local Self Government, which "promoted political and financial autonomy for local authorities".[2]

The relative decline of the influence of the state politically and economically in the international arena has thus taken place alongside a relative increase in the political and economic influence of cities, as one of a number of emerging international and transnational actors. Martins (2004: p. 2) argues that this is reflected in attempts by cities to "re-write their history free from states by carrying out their own strategies to enhance their competitive advantage", and it is against this backdrop that hosting mega-events has "emerged as a significant focus of global inter-urban competition" (Martins, 2004: p. 2). Through hosting mega-events such as the Olympic Games, cities hope to enhance their prominence as international actors in their own right. This reflects the general sense that, in diplomacy, actors are engaged in negotiating primarily to promote their own interests, whether economic, cultural or political, in the international arena. Indeed from a Realist perspective, even where diplomatic discourse concerns mediation with the objective of conflict resolution, such mediation ultimately promotes the interests of the mediating states.[3]

Conceptualizing 'Olympic diplomacy'

Use of the term 'Olympic diplomacy' to encapsulate a broad spectrum of activities carried out by a wide range of actors with an interest in the Olympic Movement, each with their own agendas, does not promote conceptual clarity. For example, much of the discourse referred to as"diplomacy' that takes place around the Olympic Games concerns states and agents of states 'using' the Games as a conduit through which to pursue particular organizational objectives (diplomacy *through* the Olympics). On the other hand, the idea that key (non-state) actors in the Olympic Movement, for example the IOC and the Organizing Committee for the Olympic Games (OCOG), can act as a mediating force between 'estranged collectives' (Der Derian, 1987) has been around for some time and essentially constitutes the diplomacy *of* the Olympics. In many contexts, the aspirations of a range of actors coincide, having a shared interest in producing and staging a 'successful' Olympic Games. Such a multi-stakeholder scenario (Hocking, 2006) is characteristic of the increasing complexity of diplomatic discourse in the global environment, where the interests of a diverse range of organizations are interdependent and where the 'public- private' dichotomy is becoming less apparent.

While acknowledging the limitations in classification, accentuating distinctions that may be more apparent than real, for the purposes of this investigation diplomacy relating to the Olympic Movement, can be understand as falling into four broad and interlocking categories These categories can be found in **Table 1** below.

Table 1   Conceptualizing Olympic Diplomacy

Categories	Actors	Activities
State diplomacy	• Foreign Affairs departments, • Trade departments • Diplomatic services	Public policy decisions on engagement (bidding / participation). Medium for development of foreign relations. Soft intelligence gathering.
Support diplomacy	• Foreign embassies, • Consular services, • Passport and immigration services	Wide range of logistical support services and hospitality for athletes and officials. Close cooperation with Chef De Mission of Olympic teams
Olympism as diplomacy	• IOC, • Olympic Sports Federations, • Regional and national Olympic Committees.	IOC generated Olympic education programmes, development programmes (Olympic Solidarity). Cultural programmes initiated at IOC and host nation levels. IOC Recognition / non-recognition of NOCs of newly emerging states
Multi-stakeholder diplomacy	• Governmental organizations at international, supranational, national and sub-national level. • Civic society organizations, sports federations, • Business and commercial organizations at local, national regional and international level.	All of the above. Also- Sub-state lobbying relating to bid and when providing services as host, involves range of business and promotional activities at local, national, regional and international level. Interest and pressure groups engaged in lobbying process.

Of the four categories, *State Diplomacy* is likely to be the most familiar to readers in that it reflects developments in geo-politics and takes place through the medium of the Games. This includes the pursuit of a range of mainstream foreign policy objectives and, at its most extreme, may involve the threat of or institution of boycotts — characteristic of diplomacy surrounding the Games of the 1980s. In relation to a bid to host the Olympics, this includes the strategic decision by a state as to whether or not it will 'back a bid'. *Support diplomacy* is an extension of traditional state diplomacy and concerns the diplomatic infrastructure that provides significant logistical support for athletes and support teams with a view to facilitating the success of the national team. Most visibly, the diplomatic attachés, seconded from the various diplomatic services world-wide, co-ordinate a framework of services including transport, accommodation and hospitality, for their national Olympic teams. At a more general level, embassies in the host city and consular services elsewhere in the host state pro-vide a number of support services. In relation to an Olympic bid this includes a range of promotional and practical support activities by embassies overseas that are supportive of the bid.

Olympism as diplomacy makes the case that the Olympic Games are to be considered in their own right as a diplomatic event. The Games thus provide an opportunity for mediation between collectives otherwise estranged perhaps as a result of foreign policy differences. One example of this was the role of the IOC in bringing together the two Koreas within the opening ceremony at the Sydney Games in 2000, subsequently presented as an example of the influence of the organisation on the international stage (Australian Bureau of Statistics, 2002). The architecture within which Olympic discourse takes place is in essence 'diplomatic'. Representatives of various organs of the Olympic Movement develop a 'diplomatic' relationship with other state and non-state actors through the bidding process, in the build up to and during the Games. The IOC as the key actor has its own agenda, which includes aspirations to play a more pro-active role in international mediation (for example, through links with the United Nations, and promotion of the Olympic Truce) and to promote its international profile, in particular through educational programmes (Binder, 2001). In addition, de facto and formal recognition by the IOC of newly emerging states can influence the process of recognition by the wider international community. In relation to the bidding process for the Olympic Games, the IOC plays a mediating role in the bid process. It has developed a sophisticated two-stage bidding framework through which it attempts to promote, by more transparent and equitable practices, better relations during the highly competitive bidding process.

Finally, *Multi-stakeholder diplomacy* is predicated on a different conception of the characteristics of actors engaged in the diplomatic process. For this category the city emerges as a key sub-state entity in diplomatic discourse relating to the Olympic Games. It operates alongside other actors with an interest in securing a successful bid to host an Olympic Games, and includes other forms of local/ regional government and local/regional and national business interests. Multi-stakeholder diplomacy concerns the activities of a multiplicity of actors with a shared interest in a particular outcome (for example, a successful Olympic bid) which at the same time provides the opportunity to secure their own competitive advantage, whether commercial, cultural or political. In this, municipal authorities and civic society organizations engage directly with a range of international actors in order to pursue their interests through the bidding process.

Diplomacy, the city and the bid

The process of bidding for the opportunity to host the Olympic Games has long generated controversy both within the Olympic Movement and among those groups hoping to secure a successful bid. It is significant in terms of diplomacy, given the perceived economic, political and place promotional benefits (Gold and Gold, 2010) of hosting the Games and the opportunities a successful bid provides for pursuing a range of sub-state as well as state level interests. The scale of the bidding process has also led to the separation of the Summer and Winter Games, which until 1992 were held in the same year. In addition, rule changes for bidding have reflected concerns with endemic corruption in the process. For example, following the controversy surrounding the bidding process for the 2002 Winter Games, when the bid committee for Salt Lake City was identified as having used a number of corrupt practices to secure the bid, a decision was taken to halt the practice of IOC officials undertaking a tour of the bidding cities (Beacom, 2004). Most significantly, rule changes to the bidding process have reflected the dramatic growth in the scale and complexity of the event, and the selection of the host city now takes place seven years prior to the staging of the Games following an initial 'applicant' phase which enables an earlier assessment when a number of contenders are eliminated (IOC, 2003).

While the prominence of a number of sub-state actors in the international diplomatic frame has been enhanced in the bidding process, the role of the state as a key actor is still generally accepted. This is despite the fact that the Olympic Charter identifies the city as the organization that must submit the bid, and does not formally require the state in question to underwrite the bid (IOC, 2010). [4] In practice however, given the increasing financial commitment required to ensure appropriate preparations are made for the Games, the capacity of the state to support the project financially is of increasing importance. It is in this regard that the state can be viewed as the only actor likely to have the resources necessary to act as guarantor. In addition, the state is the only institution with the capability to mobilise the resources necessary to ensure that the security requirements identified in the bid are met. The state has also, through its diplomatic services and extensive networks based on membership of international organizations, lobbying power critical to the bidding process. At the same time, it is well placed to influence domestic public opinion — in itself critical to the bidding process (although the capacity of interest groups to influence public opinion through the media should not be underestimated).

The dynamics of the bidding process and related diplomatic discourse continue to change as the relative influence of a variety of actors (including municipal authorities) fluctuates (for example, changing relations between central and local government).[5] Nevertheless, the status accorded to cities in international society provides particular opportunities for municipal diplomacy. Aspirations to host the Olympic Games and other international events requires active diplomatic engagement in order to secure competitive advantage in the bidding process. At the same time, future patterns of bidding for the Olympics may be very different — resulting from the escalating cost of bidding for and hosting the Games. **Table 2** indicates that the most recent high-water mark for numbers of cities bidding for the Games may have been reached with the eleven applicant cities registered at the beginning of the bidding process for the 2004 and 2008 Games. There were nine applicant cities for the 2012 Games and seven for the 2016 Games. The new Global economic challenges and mounting anxiety concerning security at this mega-event may indeed further inhibit cities engaging in this process.

The central role of the state in successful Olympic bids remains crucial. The lead taken by the state in the bidding process is evident in a number of ways. In particular, given the increasing financial commitment required to ensure appropriate preparations are made for the Games, the capacity of the state to support the project financially is of increasing importance. Additional imperatives for state

Table 2: bidding for the Olympic Games (since 1952)

Year	Bidding Cities		Winning bid / IOC session
1952	Amsterdam, Chicago Detroit, Los Angeles Minneapolis, Philadelphia		**Helsinki** (40th: Stockholm 21 June 1947)
1956	Buenos Aires, Chicago Detroit, Los Angeles Mexico City, Minneapolis Philadelphia, San Francisco		**Melbourne** (43rd : Rome 28 April 1949)
1960	Brussels, Budapest Detroit, Lausanne Mexico City, Tokyo		**Rome** (50th : Paris 15 June 1955)
1964	Brussels, Detroit Vienna		**Tokyo 55th :** (Munich 25 May 1959)
1968	Buenos Aires, Detroit Lyon		**Mexico City** (60th : Baden-Baden 18 October 1963)
1972	Detroit, Madrid Montreal		**Munich** (64th : Rome 26 April 1966)
1976	Los Angeles Moscow		**Montreal** (69th : Amsterdam 12 May 1970)
1980	Los Angeles		**Moscow** (75th : Vienna 23 October 1974)
1984	New York		**Los Angeles** (80th: Athens 18 May 1978)
1988	Nagoya		**Seoul** (84th: Baden Baden 30 September 1981)
1992	Amsterdam, Belgrade Birmingham, Brisbane, Paris		**Barcelona** (91st : 17 October 1986)
1996	Athens, Belgrade Manchester, Melbourne, Toronto		**Atlanta** (96th: Tokyo 18 September 1990)
2000	Beijing, Berlin Istanbul, Manchester		**Sydney** (101st: Monte-Carlo 23 September 1993)
2004	**Applicant cities not chosen as candidates** Istanbul, Lille Rio de Janeiro St Petersburg San Juan, Seville	**Candidate cities** Buenos Aires Cape Town Rome Stockholm	**Athens** (106th: Lausanne 5 September 1997)
2008	Bangkok, Cairo Havana Kuala Lumpur Seville	Istanbul Osaka Paris Toronto	**Beijing** (112th : Moscow 13 July 2001)
2012	Havana, Istanbul Leipzig, Rio de Janeiro	Madrid Moscow NY City, Paris	**London** (117th : Singapore 6 July 2005)
2016	Baku, Doha Prague	Chicago Madrid, Tokyo	**Rio de Janeiro** (121st : Copenhagen 2 October 2009)

support for an event of this magnitude include:

- the implications for regional and state security, given the capacity of the state to mobilize resources in response to such challenges;

- the continued lobbying power of the state internationally, in the bidding process;

- the capacity of the state to mobilize domestic public support — crucial to mounting a successful Olympic bid.

The argument concerning the continuation of the state as super-ordinate is further supported by the idea of the state attributing competencies to sub-state entities and these competencies generally determining the nature and extent of their involvement in diplomatic discourse. Only occasionally do defence or international treaties regarding issues such as shared sovereignty and territorial disputes enter the policy domain of sub-state bodies (Criekemans, 2006).[6] Such issues remain, for the most part, pre-occupations of the state and, in turn, set the context for its engagement in diplomacy. In the case of sub-state entities, such as municipal and local authorities, issues such as international profile, economic activity and cultural influence determine the parameters of their policy domain and in turn their engagement with diplomatic discourse. In similar fashion, multi-national companies become engaged in the lobbying process (demonstrating many of the characteristics of multi-stakeholder diplomacy) where it is necessary to provide representation to protect and promote strategic interests. Similarly, non-governmental groups may engage in diplomatic activity where they provide representation in support of a change in particular area of international law — for example environmental organizations lobbying to influence international environmental negotiations (Betsill and Corell, 2008).

The state then, remains the key actor in international diplomacy. It sets the terms of reference for much of the international discourse that takes place beyond traditional state parameters. Nevertheless there has been fundamental change in the international arena, reflected in the characteristics of actors engaged in diplomatic discourse. This is evidenced in the nature of diplomacy as it relates to the Olympic bid. The idea of a multiplicity of actors engaged in bidding, all with a stake in success, does appear to be the most appropriate interpretation of current developments concerning diplomatic discourse as it relates to the bid. In this sense, the multi-stakeholder model provides a framework for investigation.

Multi-stakeholder diplomacy and the Olympic bid

The lobbying process that forms part of bidding for the Olympic Games articulates the diffusion of activity central to the multi-stakeholder diplomacy model. The bid becomes a point of exchange between a range of actors — state and non-state — operating at local, regional, national and international level. Representatives of municipal authorities and local business groups can interact with national politicians, civil servants and international NGOs as they engage in lobbying that is characteristic of the bidding process. In the case of the London 2012 bid, five metropolitan Olympic Boroughs (Greenwich, Hackney, Newham, Tower Hamlets and Waltham Forest) were drawn into the lobbying process, along with the Mayor of London's Office, the London Development Agency (LDA) and a range of metropolitan, regional and national business interests. From a sports perspective, the British Olympic Association (BOA) and the national Olympic sports federations were engaged in the process, in support of the main stakeholder,'London 2012.'At the same time, government departments — in particular the Foreign and Commonwealth Office (FCO) and the Department for Culture, Media and Sport (DCMS) — were active on a number of levels. While tensions inevitably did arise during the bidding process, most stakeholders shared an interest in mounting a successful bid (notwithstanding the efforts of pressure groups such as *Nolondon2012* who lobbied against the bid on economic, community and environmental grounds).

Introducing the multi-stakeholder model, Hocking and Kelly (2002) make the point that the demands of global governance require the development of increasingly innovative diplomacy as the issues facing the global community increase in complexity. Consequently there is a tendency among the global community for authority to be diffused among its constituent actors, some of whom represent the interests of the business community. The most noteworthy of these in the UK is arguably the Chamber of Commerce. Hocking and Kelly's exploration of the Chamber of Commerce as an actor on the international stage suggests that its increasing influence is as a lobbying organization which identifies niche areas of policy and develops strategies to influence them. This has been evident since the inter-war years when it became involved in debate concerning the direction and administration of reparations and the development of a relationship with the League of Nations and the International Labour Organization. Change in the international environment has subsequently provided more room for the Chamber of Commerce to manoeuvre.

Hocking and Kelly (2002) consider, in particular, the developing relationship with the United Nations.

It is noteworthy that in the Chicago bid for the 2016 Olympic Games, intense lobbying was evident from a variety of organizations representing business interests in the city. In particular, a letter to the IOC President Jacques Rogge was sent by the Chair and President of the Chicagoland Chamber of Commerce. The letter included a strongly worded endorsement of the bid, together with a commitment to work with the municipal authorities to promote a range of measures to reduce traffic congestion during the period of the Games such as staggered work patterns and flexible use of annual leave (Chicagoland Chamber of Commerce, 2009). Again it was apparent that a network of actors operating at a variety of levels were working to the common goal of promoting the (ultimately unsuccessful) Chicago bid.

Beyond the bid — Olympic diplomacy and sub-state interests in the build-up to the Games

The chapter has already established that sub-state, including municipal, interests are represented within wider diplomatic discourse relating to the Olympic Games. In the context of commercial diplomacy, Girginov (2008) notes that the Scottish Executive published a 'Scottish Strategy for Stronger Engagement with China' in 2006. This reflected a determination by the Executive to ensure that Scotland benefited from the already significant commercial activity that was taking place between the UK and China; activity that was expected to increase in the lead-up to the Beijing Games in 2008. In the context of the London 2012 bid, presented as a bid for Britain, a concerted effort was made to highlight ways in which the home nations (England, Wales, Scotland and Northern Ireland) and regions could benefit from the Games. In this sense, it was not just the sub-state actors engaged in promoting themselves, but it was in the interest of the bid committee, and subsequently the London Organizing Committee for the Olympic Games (LOCOG) and the UK government concerned with promoting the idea of legacy, to ensure that those actors had the opportunity to benefit from the Games (Lee, 2006). A wide range of actors had then, coalesced around the 'legacy agenda'; from the IOC at a global level, through to regional municipal and local level. Mangan (2008: p. 1869) points to three reasons for the IOC pursuing legacy. First, a positive legacy "avoids the public in the host city/nation, blaming the IOC and provides evidence that the event has been good for the host city/nation". Second, it provides justification for the high spend on "permanent or temporary event infrastructure". Third, it encourages "other cities/nations to bid for future events and this increases the power of the IOC...". In relation to legacy, the IOC is the key stakeholder since successive Olympic Games without discernable legacy benefits (making a positive contribution to long term economic, social and cultural development) would be likely to erode the legitimacy of the Olympic Movement as an international entity with the capacity to contribute to development objectives. To deliver legacy however, a multiplicity of stakeholders including LOCOG, the Olympic Delivery Authority (ODA), the Government Olympic Executive (GOE), the Nations and Regions Group, the Olympic Park Legacy Company (OPLC), and many other commercial and civil society organizations, will need to engage in a well co-ordinated and appropriately resourced range of initiatives that are integral to the Games and that are self-sustaining in the longer term.

One aspect of the legacy agenda for 2012 is the development of a network of Pre-Games Training Camps (PGTCs) throughout the UK with the objective of providing long term benefits for the organizations and communities involved in their provision. The London 2012 Games were the first to develop a comprehensive framework of PGTCs. While this was initially seen as a positive aspect of the bid, a proposal from the bid committee to pay £25,000 to teams who came to the UK prior to the Games to train at a PGTC was considered as contravening regulations. Accusations of bribery quickly surfaced and threatened to derail the London bid. The offer of payment was rapidly withdrawn for the remainder of the bid process, but was reinstated subsequent to London winning the bid (LOCOG undated).

From October 2006, organizations/facilities were invited to apply for the opportunity to host PGTCs. Camps were subsequently inspected to ensure they were of a sufficient standard for use by Olympic athletes and, where appropriate, were registered. On 3 March 2008 a LOCOG press release noted that a 'record number' of sporting facilities — over 600 across Britain — had registered as pre-Olympic training venues. LOCOG indicated their intention to publish the PGTC guide at Beijing.[7] This guide was indeed published and was circulated to all NOCs and NPCs who were attending Beijing for the Games. Visit Britain, the national tourist agency, developed a new website in association with LOCOG to bring "its experience of marketing destinations and tourist products to international audiences" (East Midlands Development Agency, 2008). This provided an electronic medium through which the camps could be promoted. At the same time Jowell, Minister for the Olympics, noted that "there are no guarantees of success [for venues] just by making it into the guide.

There will be fierce competition to host foreign teams and individuals and now it is for every ... venue to sell itself internationally".[8] Nevertheless, from the perspective of the wider Olympic Movement, the initiative was viewed as a positive development. Gunilla Lindberg, Secretary General of the Association of NOCs, was quoted in the press release as indicating that she was pleased with the progress that was made in developing a framework of training facilities.

With the requirement for regional organizations to promote their own training camps, a number emerged as particularly effective in securing Olympic or Paralympic teams early in the process. In this respect, a small number of Higher Education Institutes (HEIs) were prominent in the bidding process from the onset. At times (for example in the case of the University of Bath) they operated as the sole or dominant stakeholder. At others (for example in the case of the Surrey bid) they operated alongside other key stakeholders, in particular the Local Authority.

The key question to be answered by communities considering providing training camps is: what is the reason for pursuing such a course? It is unlikely that a significant financial gain will be forthcoming. While Olympic and Paralympic teams basing themselves in the UK for the purposes of training are able to secure up to £25,000 from LOCOG to support training in registered venues, the dissemination of that funding across a range of activities and support facilities is likely to mean that its impact is negligible. The impact of other related investment and additional visitor spend has yet to be quantified, but is likely to play a limited role in the development of regional economies. Nevertheless, LOCOG is promoting such activity as central to securing a sporting and health legacy, where the presence of Olympic teams may raise the profile of sport in a locality and a range of related initiatives may act as a catalyst to increased participation levels. Again, this is a difficult area to quantify. Of greater significance is the argument that hosting Olympic and Paralympic teams, prior to the Games, provides a unique opportunity to enhance the profile of a city or region. It is in this sense that the process can be linked to the argument concerning diplomatic discourse below the level of the state, as Local Authorities alongside HEIs negotiate in the international arena to secure competitive advantage in the application process.

Beyond the Olympic Games themselves then, the separate bidding that emerges within and around London 2012, as cities and regions compete internationally for the right to host PGTCs, is significant in the sense that such negotiation by local and regional stakeholders constitutes a new aspect of Olympic diplomacy. The success or otherwise, of the London 2012 PGTC initiative will ultimately determine whether or not this approach to pre-games training arrangements becomes a feature of future Olympics Games, so leading to a longer term shift in the contours of diplomatic discourse as it relates to the Olympic Games.

Concluding thoughts

The historian H.A.L. Fisher (1936, preface) comments, "men wiser and more learned than I have discerned in history a plot, a rhythm, a predetermined history. These harmonies are concealed from me". If, as suggested by commentators on international relations and diplomacy, the state is in decline relative to other actors (Langhorne, 2005; Sharp, 2009), then this should indeed be reflected in changing patterns of diplomatic discourse in the great theatres of international diplomacy, of which the Olympic Games is one. Explaining Olympic diplomacy, in the context of an emerging pattern of discourse that focuses on the diffusion of diplomatic actors at the expense of the state, would in this sense seem appropriate. Yet experience on the ground does not appear to support this contention. Rather than a clearly identifiable pattern, there are fluctuations in the nature of such activity, dependent upon the geo-political context within which the bidding process and the Games themselves, take place. Characteristics of the host country regime, dominant themes in international politics at the time (for example, environmental and development politics as well as local and regional conflicts), the global economic situation and IOC relationships with international sports networks and governmental bodies, all influence the nature of diplomatic discourse relating to each Olympic Games. Consequently attempting to plot a linear shift in patterns of Olympic diplomacy from the 1984 Olympic Games in Los Angeles, through the 1992 Barcelona Games, the 1996 Atlanta Games and on to the 2008 Games in Beijing provides no meaningful insights into such discourse.

It would appear that there are some constants. In each case, the city is dependent on the state in order to mount a successful bid for the Olympic Games. Even here however, the role of the state is inconsistent. For example in the case of successful bids by US cities, the relationship between the bid committee and the Federal and State governments has been relatively limited. A very different picture to that experienced by European and Asiatic city bids.

Notwithstanding the challenges inherent in predicting the future of the bid and bid diplomacy however, it is likely that as cities develop territorial strategies in response to the challenges of the globalization process (characterized in this context by diffusion of authority with increasing numbers of interdependent actors engaging in economic and political activities), bidding for international events, along with other commercial and civil society stakeholders, will continue to form an important part of these strategies. Whether or not this will include bidding for the Summer Olympic and Paralympic Games is however, a rather different issue. Even with the support from the state, international sponsors and the media, the prohibitive cost of staging the Games will screen out many potential cities. There are increasing opportunities to bid for other sporting and non-sporting events that provide many of the legacy benefits associated with the Olympics, without exposing the city to such high risks. Within the wider Olympic family, the Youth Olympic Games, a variety of Olympic Festivals and the Special Olympics provide opportunities for cities to bid for and host events which, while attracting less international media attention and business activity, do require much less dependence on central government, while still providing a catalyst for social, cultural, sporting and infrastructure development that promotes the city or region on the international stage. Beyond the Olympic Family, there are opportunities to host regional and world championships in many high profile sports, again without the huge financial commitment and other risks associated with hosting the Olympic Games.

Cities continue to evolve as actors in global diplomacy and this will increasingly be articulated through the discourse relating to the competitive bidding process for international events. Municipal authorities and other stakeholders in developing states will feature more prominently in this process. The challenge for the IOC, concerned with the international reputation of the Games as a catalyst for economic and cultural development, is to ensure that the Olympics (and by association, the Paralympics) will feature as the event of choice in the face of concerns that it has outgrown itself.

Notes

1 Pluijm (2007), while developing the theme of the expanding role of 'city diplomacy', does nevertheless recognise this continued pivotal role of the state in the diplomatic process.

2 European Charter of Local Self-Government, Strasbourg, 15.X.1985 http://conventions.coe.int/Treaty/EN/Treaties/Html/122.htm (accessed 10 May 2010).

3 Realism as a branch of International Relations (IR) theory continues to identify the state as the key actor in shaping the contours of international relations. It follows that the Realist perspective on diplomacy focuses on the state as setting the terms of reference and controlling the

diplomatic process (Brown, 2005).

4   While it has become custom and practice for states to underwrite the enormous financial commitment contingent with an Olympic bid, this is not necessarily required according to the Olympic Charter. The requirement is rather, that 'Each candidate city should provide financial guarantees as required by the IOC Executive Board, which will determine whether such guarantees shall be issued by the city itself, or by other competent local, regional or national public authorities, or by any third parties'. (*IOC Olympic Charter* [2010], bye-law to Rule 34: 74).

5   Saner and Yui (2003, p. 5) refer to the German Llander and the Swiss Canton as sub-state political entities who deploy independent representation in an effort to influence for example, the process of EU policy making. This, they argue, is taking place at a time when there is a multiplicity of actors emerging on the international stage, attempting to gain competitive advantage through direct representation.

6   Criekemans (2006) notes that the federated entities that constitute the Netherlands, have indeed, the right to conclude or make treaties with third parties (e.g. sovereign states, regional organizations etc.) this is in contrast with most federations for example the USA, where the states cannot enter into such arrangements.

7   Facilities were invited to apply in July 2006. The assessment process was carried out during 2007. www.londonorg.com.pressoffice. 0203 2012100 (accessed 6 March 2010).

8   LOCOG Press Release, *Pre-Olympic Games Training* http://www. london 2012.com/press/media-releases/2008/03/over-600facilities-from-across-the-uk-appear-in-london2012–pre-games-train.php (accessed 7 March 2010).

References

Australian Bureau of Statistics (2002) *A look back at the Sydney Olympics and Paralympics*. http: //www.abs.gov.au/ausstats/ (accessed 29 April 2011).

Barston, R. (2006) *Modern diplomacy (3rd ed)*. Longman.

Baylis, J. and Smith, S. (2005) *The globalization of world politics* (3rd edn). Oxford: Oxford University Press.

Beacom, A. (2004) 'A changing discourse? British diplomacy and the Olympic Movement','in Levermore, R. and Budd, A. (eds) *Sport and international relations: An emerging relationship*. London: Routledge, pp. 93–111.

Berridge, G. (2005) *Diplomacy: Theory and practice* (3rd edn). Basingstoke: Palgrave.

Betsill, M. and Corell, E. (eds) (2008) *NGO diplomacy: The influence of non-governmental organizations in international environmental negotiations*. Cambridge MA: MIT Press.

Binder, D. (2001) '"Olympism" revisited as context for global education: Implications for physical education', *Quest* Vol. 53, No. 1: pp. 14–34.

Brown, C. (2005) *Understanding international relations* (3rd edn). Basingstoke: Palgrave.

Chicagoland Chamber of Commerce (2009) *Chamber gives Chicago's 2016 Olympic Games bid a boost.* http: //www.chicagolandchamber.org/news/archive/Pages/ChambergivesChicago (20 September 2009)

Criekemans, D. (2006) 'How sub-national entities try to develop their own paradiplomacy: The case of Flanders (1993–2005)'. Geneva: International Conference Challenges for Foreign Ministries — Managing Diplomatic Networks and Optimising Value. Online http: //www.diplomacy.edu/Conferences/MFA/papers/criekemans.pdf (17 August 2010)

Der Derian, J. (1987) *On diplomacy: A genealogy of Western estrangement.* London: Blackwell.

East Midlands Development Agency (3 March 2008) *Press release: Top East Midlands aports facilities to be included in London 2012 Pre-Games Training Camp Guide* http: //www.emda.org.uk/news/newsreturn.asp?fileno=3337 (accessed 30 April 2011)

European Charter of Local Self-Government, Strasbourg, 15.X.1985 http://conventions.coe.int/Treaty/EN/Treaties/Html/122.htm (accessed 10 may 2010).

Fisher, H. (1936) *A history of Europe.* London: Edward Arnold and Co.

Girginov, V. (June 2008) 'Creative tensions: 'Join in London' meets 'Dancing Beijing' — The cultural power of the Olympics', *The International Journal of the History of Sport,* Vol. 25, No. 7, pp. 893–914

Girginov, V. and Hills, L. (2008) 'A sustainable sports legacy: Creating a link between the London Olympics and sports participation', *The International Journal of the History of Sport* Vol. 25, No. 14, pp. 2091–2116.

Gold, J. and Gold, M. (2010) 'Olympic cities: Regeneration, city rebranding and changing urban agendas', Girginov, V. (ed) *The Olympics: A critical reader.* Abingdon: Routledge.

Hocking, B. (2006) 'Multistakeholder diplomacy: Foundations, forms, functions and frustrations', in Kurbalija, J. and Katrandjiev, V. (eds) *Multistakeholder diplomacy: Challenges and opportunities.* Malta/Geneva: Diplofoundation 2006, pp. 13–29.

Hocking, B and Kelly, D. (2002) 'Doing business? The International Chamber of Commerce, the United Nations, and the Global Compact', in Cooper, A., English, J. and Thakur, R. (eds) *Enhancing global governance: Towards a new diplomacy?.* New York: United Nations University Press.

Hocking, B and Spence, D. (2002) *Foreign mnistries in the European Union: Integrating diplomats.* London: Palgrave Macmillan.

IOC (2003) *Candidature Acceptance Procedure: Games of the XXX Olympiad 2012.* Lausanne: IOC.

—————— (2010) *The Olympic Charter.* Lausanne: IOC

—————— (2009a) *The Olympic Movement* http: //www.olympic.org/uk/organisation/index_uk.asp (05 September 2009).

—————— (2009b) *Report of the 2016 IOC Evaluation Commission.* PDF (accessed 25 October 2010)

Jinxia, D. and Mangan, J. (2008) 'Beijing Olympics Legacies: Certain intentions and certain and uncertain outcomes', *The International Journal of the History of Sport* Vol. 25, No. 14, pp. 2019–2040.

Langhorne, R. (June 2005) 'The diplomacy of non-state actors', *Diplomacy and Statecraft Vol.* 16, No. 2 331–339.

LOCOG (undated) *Preparing for 2012: Financial Contributions Guidelines.* LOCOG_pgtc_financial_contribution_guidelines.pdf (accessed 20 September 2010)

LOCOG Press Release, *Pre-Olympic Games Training* http://www.london 2012.com/press/media-releases/2008/03/over-600 facilities-from-across-the-uk-appear-in-london2012–pre-games-train.php (accessed 7 March 2010)

Lee M. (2006) *The race for the 2012 Olympics: The inside story of how London won the bid.* London: Virgin.

Leonard, M. (2002) *Public diplomacy.* London: The Foreign Policy Centre.

London Organizing Committee for the Olympic Games (undated) *Preparing for 2012, Pre-Games Training Camps: Financial Contributions Guidelines* LOCOG_pgtc_financial_contribution_guidelines[1].pdf (accessed 29 April 2011)

Macrury, I. and Poynter, G. (December 2008) 'The regeneration games: Commodities, gifts and the economics of London 2012', *The International Journal of the History of Sport* Vol. 25, No. 14, pp. 2072–2090.

Mangan, J. A. (2008) 'Prologue: Guarantees of global goodwill: Post-Olympic legacies — too many limping white elephants?', *International Journal of the History of Sport* Vol. 25, No. 4: pp. 1869–1883.

Martins, L. (2004) Conference paper, 'Bidding for the Olympics, a local sffair? Lessons learned from the Paris and Madrid 2012 Olympic bids', *City Futures Conference* 8–10 July, Chicago University College of Urban Planning and Public Affairs.

Melissen J. (2007) *The new diplomacy: Soft power in international relations.* Basingstoke: Palgrave.

Pluijm, R. (2007) 'City diplomacy: The expanding role of cities in international politics', *Clingendael Diplomacy Papers No. 10.* The Hague: Netherlands Institute of International Relations. Online. www.clingendael.nl/publications/2007/20070400_cdsp_paper_pluijm.pdf (4 October 2010)

Reinecke, W. (1998) *Global public policy: Governing without government?* Washington D.C.: Brookings Institution Press.

Ruggie (2005) 'Modernists must take over the United Nations', *Financial Times,* 24 January.

Saner, R. & Yui, L. (January 2003) 'International Economic Diplomacy: Mutations in Post-Modern Times'. *Netherlands Institute of International Relations: Discussion paper no. 84.* Online www.csend.org/component/docman/doc_download/48–dp-dsppdfc (accessed 2 October 2010).

Sharp, P. (1999) 'For diplomacy: Representation and the study of international relations', *International Studies Association* Vol. 1, Part 1: pp. 33–57.

———— (2009) *Diplomatic theory of international relations*. Cambridge: Cambridge University Press.

Tatham, M. (2010) 'With or without you? Revisiting territorial state-bypassing in EU interest representation', *Journal of European Public Policy* Vol. 17, No. 1: pp. 76–99.

Watson, A. (1982) *Diplomacy: The dialogue between states*. London: Methuen Ltd.

———— (1992) *The evolution of international society*. London: Routledge.

THE SHIFTING DYNAMICS OF LOCAL GOVERNMENT SPORTS DEVELOPMENT OFFICER PRACTICE IN ENGLAND: NEW IDENTITIES AND HAZY PROFESSIONAL BOUNDARIES

Chris Mackintosh

Nottingham Trent University, England

Introduction

For those working in sports development there is a potentially blurred sense of professional identity and an increasingly complex wider notion of a shared field of 'professional practice' (see Hylton and Hartley, this volume, for a detailed discussion). This is not to suggest that a unified, coherent and unambiguous professional identity can actually exist in community sports development. The purpose of this research is to examine the field of public sector practice in sports development in ten local authority settings in England. In recent policy shifts there has arguably been a movement to refocus on national governing bodies of sport (NGBs) and County Sports Partnerships (CSPs) over traditional delivery agents such as the local authority (Houlihan, 2011; Mackintosh, 2011; Sport England, 2008). Whilst 'sports development' is a notoriously hard field to define and delineate (Bloyce and Smith, 2010; Houlihan and White, 2002; Hylton, 2010; Hylton and Bramham, 2008), this research project explores sports development officer (SDO) professional practice and the challenges facing these public sector workers in local authority settings in England. In recent times some attention has been given to the role of the SDO in relation to organisational change in England (Bloyce et al., 2008) and attempts to re-conceptualise practice (Bolton et al., 2008). However, given the scale of this sphere of public service provision, much remains to be learned about local authority SDO professional practice. Some exceptions to this include analysis of managers in CSPs in the East Midlands (Mackintosh, 2011), local authority development officers in Liverpool (King, 2009), local authority sports development practice in Blaenau Gwent (Bolton et al., 2008) and SDOs in North West England (Bloyce et al., 2008).

113

An earlier industry estimate pitched the number of SDOs in the UK at between 2,500 and 3,000 (Collins, 1995). It has been estimated by a study undertaken for Skills Active in 2004 that, since 1995 there had been between 4,000 and 5,000 people in full time or part time employment in this sector in the United Kingdom (Pitchford, 2005). Since this time the sports development sector has seen further expansion and the number of people currently working in the field is unknown.

For the purpose of this chapter, analysis is given over to those working in public sector local authority settings. However, it is at times difficult to separate out those others who are working in physical education (PE) settings, sports coaching and sports management and who could also be deemed to be contributing towards sports development objectives. For example, many PE teachers have been actively engaged with School Sport Partnership (SSP) work and club links that were core to recent sports development delivery led by Sport England. But recent changes by the new coalition government in England have minimised the work of SSPs, abolished Sports Colleges, and cut Sport England funding by around 30%: these changes will have clear implications for employment in the sector. In contrast, sports development experienced a period of relative growth and expansion under the New labour administration since its election in 1997. [Note that the fieldwork for this project was undertaken prior to the comprehensive spending review cuts announced in 2010].

As has been well documented, there is also a wide network of volunteers who actively engage with areas of sports development practice but who will not appear in any total figure as they are not directly 'employed' in this area of professional practice (Nichols *et al.*, 2001, Nichols *et al.*, 2003). Given the expansion of networks under New Labour from 1997 to 2010 through SSPs, CSPs and other initiatives such as Further Education School Sports Co-ordinators (FESCOs) it can be expected that the size of the SDO employment field has expanded even further since the Active Skills study in 2004. Other authors have also recognised the widening of the scope of the work of the 'traditional' SDO into fields such as youth work, probation work and health promotion work where sport is used as a vehicle for delivering a range of social welfare agenda targets (Coalter, 2007; Coalter, 2007a; Hylton and Totten, 2008; Nichols, 2004; Smith and Waddington, 2004). Thus, the typical framing and identification of the limits of sports development are highly problematic and would perhaps even be seen as unhelpful in recognising the diverse scope of this field.

In other areas of public service practice there has been considerable attention given to developing a critical and research-informed practice (teaching/education, social care, and probation work). In parallel to these research-informed movements in other areas, sports development has attracted minimal academic appraisal that tries to evaluate and shape the notion of evidence-based practice (Smith and Leech, 2010). This is not to say that academic researchers have not identified limitations in the evidence base behind policy rhetoric (Coalter, 2007; Long *et al.*, 2001). However, the need to develop a more rigorous understanding and insight into the development of professional practice and emerging professional identities is long overdue. Indeed the artificial separation of policy, politics and practice is a problematic process and one with its own inherent dilemmas (Hill, 2005). But, refocusing upon practice, the delivery of practitioners is essential to informing our understanding of sports development. In part this research aims to address this current gap in knowledge and encourage others to develop a more critical insight into SDO practice. This paper will examine and critique the existing literature underpinning this area of research, outline the rationale and process of the research methodology, and then go on to present the findings that emerged from the research.

Research questions

This research set out with the following central questions:

- How does the local authority SDO negotiate a sense of their professional identity?
- How is the role of the local authority SDO changing and reacting to current policy priorities?
- What are SDO attitudes to the potential use of research and evidence-based practice?

Sports development practice and policy: A contested theoretical domain?

Sports development policy has attracted increasing attention in recent years (Bloyce and Smith, 2010; Green, 2005; Girginov, 2008; Houlihan and Green; 2005; Houlihan and White, 2002). However, local practice and the associated range of different dimensions have been critically appraised to a far lesser extent (King, 2009). Indeed, it has been specifically recognised that there is a lack of published research at the local authority sports development level (King, 2009). This point reflects what Green (2005) identifies as an under-theorised area of sports management practice. The very notion of 'practice' is examined or defined in minimal detail in the sports development literature: more common are historical appraisals of the different policy changes over time and changes in government approaches to sports development (Houlihan and White, 2002). Other work claims that practice could be aligned with delivery, implementation and conceptualised alongside the management of an emerging profession (Girginov, 2008). Furthermore, other examples of recent work by Collins (2010) have taken a case study approach to examining a range of professional delivery spheres in community sports development practice. Here, attempts are made to contextualise volunteer management, club development and other aspects of delivery, underpinned with recognition of the role research can play in such practice.

The academic literature investigating the work of the SDO as a professional is also minimal, but also builds a case for the need for further research into the professional identity, field of delivery and aspects of contemporary sport provision in the UK. This point is supported by the view that although "there is a growing body of literature on the ways and extent to which sport development is changing, there have been few attempts to examine the consequences of this for those charged with implementing those changes: namely, SDOs" (Bloyce *et al.*, 2008: p. 360).

As has been recognised elsewhere, the focus upon promoting sports participation is a central characteristic of the profession (Bolton *et al.*, 2008; Hylton and Totten, 2008; Mackintosh, 2011). Bolton *et al.* (2008) also point to the importance of participation promotion work to all sport and leisure professionals. Historically, earlier SDO work might have been aligned to further specialisation with minority and target group populations such as identified ethnic minority communities (Snape and Binks, 2008) or women and girls and the disabled (Hylton and Totten, 2008). But it could be argued that, with macro policy changes and shifts towards recent health-led agendas, this historical professional focus is evolving and changes in the patterns of SDO delivery may also be shifting (Bloyce and Smith, 2010; Snape and Binks, 2008).

In their research with SDOs in the north west of England, Bloyce *et al.* (2008) uncovered a trend towards SDOs themselves defining their profession as being closely aligned with the sometimes competing policy domains of increasing mass participation and the nurturing and developing of talented individuals in sport.

Furthermore, SDOs also identified and reflected upon governmental shifts towards sport as a vehicle for social change in areas such as crime prevention and healthy lifestyle promotion. There is a growing literature critically analysing the evidence base of such policy rhetoric (Coalter, 2007; Houlihan and White, 2002; Long *et al.*, 2001; Nichols, 2007). For those tasked with delivery, the implications of such changes are equally significant and yet currently under-examined.

A central argument presented as to the changing nature of SDO professional practice is the importance of partnership working (Bloyce *et al.*, 2008; Bolton *et al.*, 2008; Lindsey, 2006; Mackintosh; 2011; Robson, 2008). This imperative could be seen as part of the wider context of the New Labour political project which has promoted partnership as a central feature of its modern architecture of government (Balloch and Taylor, 2000; Dowling *et al.*, 2004; Glendinning *et al.*, 2002). As Bloyce *et al.* (2008:p. 371) recognise through the field work they undertook with SDOs, "there is now an emerging expectation that SDOs in local authorities will work with a range of partners such as County Sports Partnerships, sports clubs, youth organizations and other community-based organisations to achieve their policy outcomes". Bloyce *et al.* (2008) also make clear that this may be as part of a wider necessity to survive as a non-statutory area of public provision. This will also have ramifications for how SDOs work in practice. King (2009) recognised that such macro level aspirations to work in partnership can be challenging as there are deeply embedded interests and priorities alongside a capacity to resist change. King (2009: p. 166) specifically highlights partnerships between sport and health where there is a "paucity of published research that accounts for the overlap between these policy areas".

Promoting sports participation and liaising with a range of community partners are two potential central areas of professional practice for the SDO. A good example of this is highlighted by Bloyce *et al.* (2008) where they recognise a shift from 'tracksuits to suits', delivery to administration and the job's requirement for bureaucracy. Other authors have also suggested that the SDO is increasingly removed from the community welfare and community development work that have previously been core features of their work (Bolton *et al.*, 2008; Hylton and Totten, 2008). This is not to suggest that community development work is no longer significant to the work of sports development but identifies a possible area of conflict to be explored. Bolton *et al.* (2008) in their research with SDOs in Blaenau Gwent in Wales explored this in detail with such practitioners considering the range of diverse approaches that can be taken to engage in sports development. Here it is pinpointed that "professionals are still seen to occupy different and distinct responsibilities and roles in the delivery and development of sport" (Bolton *et al.*, 2008: p. 98). It may be that the SDO now sits at a difficult nexus between direct engagement with those communities they aspire to influence and an increasingly distant administration-led role. Bolton *et al.* (2008) also argue that notions of community need to be refocused upon and placed at the centre of practice, a point reiterated by some of the more experienced sports development practitioners in their research project. Their conceptualisation arguably benefits from the synergy of academic and practitioners within the research project authorship. This is increasingly rare but potentially necessary for clearer understanding of the synergy between theory and practice (Mackintosh *et al.*, 2010).

A useful attempt to explore a theme within sports development practice is that of Lindsey (2008) where the sustainability of programmes and the role of theory in informing understanding and delivery around this theme are considered. Here, it is argued that much like the partnership working mentioned earlier, far greater understanding and clarity is needed to improve practice in this area of the sports development profession. In particular, Lindsey looks beyond the prescribed boundaries of the SDO towards health promotion project delivery to utilise theoretical frameworks that could inform our understanding of an application in sports development. Here, it is argued that further research is needed to understand the different types of sustainability that could be considered and the linkages between effectiveness and sustainability. Where such a future project could overlap is in a deeper analysis of the SDOs and their role in shaping such features of practice. Lindsey (2008) recognises the limitations of the degree of control the SDO may have over sustainability processes. Whether this points towards earlier shifts related to the changing nature of their professional practice experienced by the SDOs interviewed by Bloyce *et al.* (2008) will be explored in this study. For example, SDOs need to shape projects, influence delivery and influence future sustainability, but instead they have perhaps become increasingly distant from this delivery.

Evidence-based practice in public sector sports development

The potential of developing more reflective professional practice in sports development could be seen as linking into the wider movement and calls for 'evidence-based practice' (Davies *et al.*, 2000; Nutley, 2007; Rowe, 2009). It has been argued that this momentum paralleled the 1997 New Labour government modernisation programme of public sector services under what has been described as a 'Third Way' ideological stance (Giddens, 1997). For others, the 'what matters is what works' mantra could be seen as a clear retreat from political ideology in itself (Davies *et al.*, 2000; Sanderson, 2002). However, in the case of sports development, much of the attention given over to research in this area has focused on policy as opposed to practice. Certainly, Sport England (2005) has begun to embrace this notion and have a comprehensive macro level research programme to evaluate and underpin policy on sports development. One exception to this is the research undertaken by Smith and Leech (2010) examining the role of research and evidence gathering within an SSP programme in England. Here, the validity and effective use of research survey data was questioned through an analysis of the experiences of PE and sports development practitioners. For many of these practitioners, evidence-based practice was viewed as top-down target chasing rather than developing research evidence to inform practice in a more meaningful way. In this study it was also identified that further research is needed in this sector to examine the role of evidence and research in more depth.

Nutley *et al.* (2007) identify three broad frameworks for under-standing and conceptualising how the use of research can be improved to inform practice. The three broad frameworks are the research-based practitioner model, the embedded research model, and an organisa-tional excellence model. Here, it is recognised that each of the three proposed models are in many ways implicit as opposed to explicit. Whilst used initially by the researchers in relation to social care they are also recognised as having potential for application in a range of public sector service provision fields. It is here, that they could be used in understanding where research is being located within sports development practice. Whilst each model has its own characteristic features Nutley *et al.* (2007) also identify that the application of these archetypes can take a form of hybrid development in practice with elements of each featuring in professionals' explicit use of research to inform their work. Which of these may fit with sports development and public sector sports evaluation and research activity will be explored later in this paper.

Methodology

This research project centred upon local authority SDO practitioners in the east midlands region of England. In total, ten SDOs were interviewed from local authority settings. This sample of professionals comprised seven men and three female workers ranging from 22 to 53 in age, and ranged from individuals in their first sports development post to others who had up to 30 years experience. The numeric bias in numbers towards men over women reflects the gender imbalance in local authority SDO practitioners across the region. The ten selected authorities were chosen based upon willingness to participate in the study and to ensure they encompassed a geographical spread across four CSP regions. The sample of professionals also ranged from one authority's lone SDO through to individuals from larger teams in urban and rural settings. The anonymity of all research participants has been preserved in the findings.

A qualitative approach to the research was undertaken as this methodology allows deep exploration of attitudes, opinions and feelings (Silverman, 2009) and gives greater scope for meeting the research aims established for this study. In-depth semi-structured interviews were used to elicit responses around selected themes. A proforma interview schedule used to guide the discussions allowed sufficient scope to explore emergent themes that offered new insights and fresh perspectives on this research area, which has to date only had limited attention (Bloyce *et al.*, 2008). Themes were shaped from the literature review, encompassing topics such as professional background, exper- ience of sports development practice, the role of research and evalua- tion, evidence-based practice, and wider changes in the profession. All interviews were transcribed verbatim to allow for thematic coding of the responses and for the interview text to be broken-down and analysed in detail (Coffey and Atkinson, 1996). All respondents were given the opportunity to terminate their involvement in the research project at any point, and ethical consideration was given to the setting, approach and data collection techniques. It is recognised that the study does have limitations. In particular, the diversity of structural and organisational settings that sports development now encompasses means that a focus on local authorities may generate too narrow an insight into the shifts being experienced. It also only examined local authority SDOs in the East Midlands region and could generate bias by not taking a wider geographical spread of subjects. Finally, further research into this area may want to examine shifts and trends by sub- sectors within the sports development field.

Research findings

The role of evidence and research in practice

The research took place during March and April 2010 in the lead-up to the UK general election. At this point respondents were already very aware of the potential funding cuts on the public sector horizon and the need to 'ensure survival'. The importance of researcher sensitivity and respondent anonymity was crucial here as many SDOs felt that either their own employment or their wider sport and leisure services team was under direct threat. One SDO summed up her position on future challenges:

> "You have to hit those agendas because there is a 15% cut coming next year...there is a vulnerability, you have to have the evidence to say what you are doing to impact on the corporate plan." [SDO, female, 28]"

Such insecurity and concern was mirrored by most respondents in this project. Alongside the broad concerns for sports development as a field of public sector practice a counter discourse was building: that of the need to measure, justify and provide evidence. This parallels other research undertaken in this sector that questioned the evidence base developed within SSP research that became more focused on delivering targets through form-filling than engaging with genuinely informative research (Smith and Leech, 2010). Arguably, calls for evidence-based policy and practice have been around for some time (Davies *et al.*, 2000; Nutley, 2007; Mackintosh, 2011; Rowe, 2009). However, evidence as seen in the quote above was less a recognition of the positive role research can play in shaping practice, and more a way to resist potential changes. In some ways in line with the findings of Smith and Leech (2010), this indicates a lack of resonance with the three archetypes of how research can be used to inform and improve public practice. Instead it perhaps fits with what Nutley (2007) identifies as potential hybrid models where, with use of research as a tool to resist change, there may be a cross over with the embedded research model. There was also a further tension with further SDOs recognising their own professional limitations with regard to planning, undertaking and interpreting research and evaluation work. As one SDO illustrated:

> "We do rely a lot on Active People surveys, but we could do more local level research. Again it is about having the capacity and the skills to do that... it would be fantastic to go and do the research with the people on the front line and hear what people are saying but that is very time expensive, going out and planning it and evaluating it." [SDO manager, male, 25]

Rowe (2009) argues for the central role Active People surveys can play in shaping a research and evidence based policy and practice in sports development. Indeed this SDO highlights the increasing importance of the national Sport England led Active People survey, but perhaps also a reliance upon it. However, perhaps more significant, it is the local capacity for research and evidence-building in terms of skills and time that may be lacking for this SDO. Another SDO, when asked directly what constraints there were on the use of research to develop evidence based practice, answered:

> "My own professional knowledge, it's not a skill I have, but it's becoming more and more prevalent and in more sound ways. You need to justify can you prove it has improved health? How can you without being very intrusive? A councillor wants to be able to say I've improved these families' health. They don't smoke etc. It's an activity with 50 kids so how has that improved family cohesion — it's hard to say. How has that stopped kids stealing cars? It's not an exact science. Is it a fallacy? To prove it is very difficult, as I guess it's a combination of factors. But the government wants to know — that's what they want!" (Senior SDO, male, 33)

Here, it is clear that this SDO sees a gap in his own professional knowledge, despite having worked in sports development for 15 years. Equally, the complexity of contemporary cross-cutting agendas further compounds the research impact measurement and evidencing process. Research and evaluation is indeed a case of 'fuzzy pictures and clear snapshots' (Coalter, 2007). What this research indicated was a gap between the vision of government for public sector sports research and evaluation and the day-to-day reality of those who would commission, undertake or plan such projects around their work programmes. The paradox here was the necessity of using research quite instrumentally to justify sports development in the current funding climate, contrasted with gaps in practitioner confidence to conduct genuinely robust research. Indeed none of the three models of research-informed practice in public services proposed by Nutley (2007) fitted the experiences highlighted in this project. But perhaps the findings of this research indicate a use of research partially embedded in practice but also to instrumentally justify, protect and support sports development services. It was admitted by several SDOs that their research skills were limited, their experiences of using research in any active way rare, and the occurrence of embedded research within day-to-day practice the exception rather than a necessity of professional practice.

Changing nature of local authority sports development

Clearly, funding cuts and changes in public sector sports development provision were on the horizon with the public sector deficit present within England. However, other knock-on effects were also being felt. For example, one SDO identified that with the National Health Service (NHS) stopping commissioning work in certain areas this was having a direct impact on what and how they deliver:

> "The local authority SDO is having to cover so many different areas, they are having to dabble with health, dabble with actually getting more people physically active. What time can they spare to be talking to specific sports and specific sports clubs about those issues. You'd be asking an awful lot of a person". [Sports Development Unit [SDU]manager, male, 50]

This was especially evident in relation to the health and physical activity agenda field where activities such as health walks, GP referral, exercise on prescription, and mental health user sports activity groups were coming under threat. Clearly, many of these activities lie outside the traditional club, school and leisure centre 'sport' nexus, but show how sports development has had to adapt and shape itself to recent New Labour agendas. This is further supported by the argument presented by a manager who comented:

> "For the first time we are staging a mass participation event [...] a Race for Life event, so 3,500 ladies will do that in July. We wouldn't have done that two or three years ago as we are too ingrained with working with clubs, coaches and schools. Well that's not the remit anymore, it's the man or woman on the street aware that they aren't as physically active as they should be." (SDU manager, male, 50)

The issue for the SDOs working in such areas was the potential impact on their communities and the loss of trust that had been built to engage and then deliver initiatives. As has been stated elsewhere, effective sports development partnerships have communication and trust at the heart of their work (Mackintosh, 2008; 2011). Losing such aspects of their partnership working may be critical for developing the localism and volunteer-led activities that the new conservative-liberal coalition government in England are arguing for.

Although there was confusion regarding the professional identity of what constituted an SDO in local authority settings, there was also contrasting clarity regarding how SDOs saw the broader purpose and philosophy behind what they do. A comment that mirrors other similar views expressed was that:

> "What we do is more people focused; most of our work is about developing the community and the people. That's what I like to think I do." (SDO, male, 33)

Similarly, another female SDO commented upon the historic shifts in the nature of sports development work that are agenda driven:

> "Making a difference, I would like that to be more central and sport for sports sake to be more central. We now have themes we are aligned to, different government agendas, crime, health, obesity and families. So no longer is sport accepted. We have to buy into those things to ensure we still exist." (SDO, female, 29)

Community and the local sports networks of the communities they work in and around were of central importance to all but two of the ten SDOs interviewed. What differed for them was the level of actual engagement and direct contact they perceived they had with their communities. As has been observed by Bloyce *et al.* (2008) in their study of SDO organisational change, there has been a movement away from track-suited delivery staff to project managers in suits. This also links to the work of Bolton *et al.* (2008) mentioned earlier that recognised a need to reposition community-focused work at the heart of the work of those in sports development. Indeed, alongside organisational change, the regularity of shifts in policy and practice expectations reported by those interviewed in this project was the one ironic constant within their profession. These findings support others in this area of research (Bloyce *et al.*, 2008; Bolton *et al.*, 2008; King, 2009).

SDO professional identity and roles

SDOs work in a complex and changing area of public sector professional practice where they frequently work across public, private and voluntary sectors and through fields including social welfare, physical activity development, sport and inclusion. As stated earlier, clear delineation of what constitutes an SDO is far from straightforward. While this project focused specifically upon the work of the local authority SDO, it is important to also recognise the variety of other organisational contexts that merge with sports development. This adds a further tier of complexity to professional identity that was beyond the scope of this research project. Findings in this research project paralleled other academic perspectives that what an SDO may constitute is now highly contested (Hylton, 2010). As one SDO stated:

> "I have been an SDO, I have defined myself as an SDO, the biggest question is what is an SDO? Nobody has ever been able to define and quantify that, because it's an ever changing thing as we've said." [Senior SDU Manager male, 50]

A further paradox with SDO identity is seen in the following quote by another SDO:

> "At the moment I do see myself as a sports development professional. I do see the value of the things we mentioned earlier and ... I do see that as an important role, as a professional role. But I don't think the people in the wider context would see that. When you go for car insurance it's never listed as a profession; never sports development officer, that one never comes up." [SDO, female, 26]

Here, it is clear that the definition of role, practice boundaries and identity change rapidly and that this is nothing new to those in the 'profession'. The point raised above in relation to status and whether sports development is a profession at all has in itself been highly contested (Hylton, 2010). This is part of a wider academic discussion beyond the remit of this paper. However, what is apparent is that the term means something to the participants in this project, but the (un)clarity of its usage and multiplicity of meanings is also evident. Another early to mid-career SDO remarked:

> "We develop sport, but we develop health, we develop participation. Yes we still use the term but it is more [than that] because people use the term at us rather than us using it." [SDU Manager, male, 35]

Crucially, here the SDO acronym is a 'term' not a clear professional identity — but one that he does embrace. This quote also reaffirms the earlier point made about the increasingly wide scope of the role of the SDO. This corresponds with earlier research undertaken by Bloyce *et al.* (2008) in the north west of England with SDOs who recognised the widening agendas of crime prevention, community safety and health promotion that now regularly fall within the remit of an SDO. Perhaps most interesting from a local government management perspective was the view expressed by one SDO who suggested:

> "... even in our leisure centres...what do you lot in sports development do? Because you can't see it. SDO identity is not clear. Does an SDO even exist anymore?" [SDO, female, 28]

Maybe the SDO no longer exists in anything more than name, or as a 'term' that people use "at" the local authority SDO. The above quote also pinpoints the local dynamics of public sports provision between facility management and sports development. Tensions seem to exist to the extent that communication may be very minimal and the perceived unquantifiable nature of sports development practice leaves a challenge for those who work in it.

Conclusions

This research project has set out to consider three key research questions around the changing role of the local authority SDO practitioner; how SDOs negotiate a sense of their own professional identity; and to examine attitudes towards the role of evidence-based practice and research in sports development. As has been noted in other studies there is limited understanding of the local authority SDO practice (Bloyce *et al.*, 2008; King, 2009). Others have likewise argued that sports development remains an under-theorised area of sports management (Green, 2005). What has emerged from this study is a picture of local authority provision as one that is in an almost constant state of flux between evolving governmental agendas. The instability and variations in scope of the work of the individual local authority SDOs means that demarking a clear field of sports development is increasingly difficult. The SDOs who contributed to this research project have to accommodate this change whilst developing their understanding of an increasingly diverse knowledge base and shifts in delivery expectations. For some, this clearly generates frustrations and creates a distance from what they perceive as the more traditional role of sports development. This traditional sphere of sports clubs, coach development, school-based events and supporting voluntary networks is a competing priority with the health, crime prevention and welfare agendas that emerged under New Labour. This finding parallels that of an earlier study of changing SDO organisational priorities conducted by Bloyce *et al.* (2008). This tension is compounded by what several SDOs saw as the genuine remit of their role, and has implications for their professional identities. It also leaves the SDOs a long way from refocusing on the community aspect of their work, as called for by Bolton *et al.* (2008) in their conceptualisation of sports development.

It is also clear that practitioners in sports development within the ten local authorities in this research project recognise the evolving importance of the research agenda within their work. However, what is also present with the findings of this study are the limitations they face in implementing notions of evidence-based practice in reality. Research for many is a low priority and in some cases a considerable challenge to their existing skills base. This is principally due to time pressures, constraints in terms of their own research skills and knowledge and perhaps reliance upon national data sets such as the Active People survey. None of the three models of research-informed practice proposed by Nutley (2007) directly fitted with the role of research in practice of the SDO practitioners in this study. But a further hybrid archetype is proposed from this research which extends the embedded research practice model into a role for justifying and protecting service provision. Given the additional financial and resource constraints being placed on local authorities through the Comprehensive Spending Review (CSR) in October 2010 (announced after the fieldwork was conducted) it may be that research becomes even less of a priority. Equally, use of research to resist change and to instrumentally evidence the achievements of a sports development service area may become a more common emergent aspect of practice.

As has been argued by other authors, there are some significant theoretical gaps in understanding and conceptualising of changes in fields of practice and knowledge in sports development (Bolton *et al.*, 2008; Green, 2005; Lindsay, 2008). This research project has begun to develop understanding of sports development practice and professional identity at local authority level that has to date remained under-examined (Bloyce *et al.*, 2008; King, 2009). Whilst opportunities for developing more research-informed practice are clear, the skills and willingness of the SDO to undertake such work is a clear challenge for the future. How sports development practice continues to realign post-New Labour across all sectors of delivery is one of the more interesting yet complex and demanding research areas to be explored under the New Coalition government. Similarly, new vehicles for delivery and implementation operating outside local government will emerge and challenge the local models of past practice. Private sector organisations, coaching consortiums and trusts may become new 'homes' for the SDO. But whether this will simply generate more confused and fragmented notions of a professional identity and compound existing challenges in delivering support for clubs, schools, and the fabric of local community sport, remains to be seen. For the practitioners in this project, SDO professional identity is most commonly and most closely bound to the sports communities they serve, not to the next modernisation process, new 'agenda' or partnership they have to develop.

References

Balloch, S. and Taylor, M. (2000) *Partnership working: Policy and practice.* Bristol, Policy Press.

Bolton, N., Fleming, S. and Elias, B. (2008) 'The experience of community sport development: A case study of Blaenau Gwent', *Managing Leisure* Vol. 13, No. 2: pp. 92–103.

Bloyce, D. and Smith, A. (2010) *Sport policy and development: An introduction.* London: Routledge.

Bloyce, D., Smith, A., Mead, R. And Morris, J. (2008) 'Playing the game (plan): A figurational analysis of organisational change in sports development in England', *European Sport Management Quarterly* Vol. 8, No. 4: pp. 359–378.

Coalter, F. (2007) *A wider social role for sport: Who's keeping the score?.* London: Routledge.

Coalter, F. (2007a) 'Sports clubs, social capital and social regeneration: "Ill-defined interventions with hard to follow outcomes"?', *Sport in Society: Cultures Commerce, Media, Politics* Vol. 10, No. 4: pp. 537–559.

Coffey, A. and Atkinson, P. (1996) *Making sense of qualitative data: Complementary research strategies.* London: Sage.

Collins, M. (1995) *Sports development locally and regionally.* Reading: Institute of Leisure and Amenity Management.

Collins, M. (2010) *Examining sports development.* London: Routledge.

Davies, H.T.O., Nutley, S. M. and Smith, P.C. (eds) (2000) *What works? Evidence-based policy and practice in public services.* Bristol, The Policy Press.

Dowling, B., Powell, M. and Glendinning, C. (2004) 'Conceptualising successful partnerships', *Health and social care in the community* Vol. 12, No. 4: pp. 309–317.

Edwards (1999) 'Reflective practice in sports management', *Sports Management Review* Vol. 2, No. 1: pp. 67–82.

Giddens, A. (1997) *The third way: The renewal of social democracy,* Cambridge, Polity.

Girginov, V. (2008) *Management of sports development.* Oxford, Butterworth-Heinemann.

Glendinning, C., Powell, M. And Rummery, K. (2002) *Partnerships, New Labour and the governance of welfare.* Bristol, Policy Press.

Green, C. B. (2005) 'Building sport programs to optimize athlete recruitment, retention, and transition: Toward a normative theory of sport development', *Journal of Sport Management* Vol. 19, No. 3: pp. 233–253.

Hill, M (2005) *The public policy process.* Harlow, Pearson Education.

Houlihan, B. (2011) 'Sport in times of austerity', paper presented at the Political Studies Association Conference, University of Birmingham March 18th 2011.

Houlihan, B. and Green, M. (2005) *Elite sports development: policy learning and political priorities.* London: Routledge.

Houilhan, B. and White, A. (2002) *The politics of sports development.* London: Routledge.

Hylton, K. (2010) 'Sports development: A profession in waiting?'.This volume.

Hylton, K. and Bramham, P. (2008) *Sports development: Policy, process and practice.* London: Routledge.

Hylton, K. and Totten, M. (2008) 'Community sports development' in Hylton, K. and Bramham, P. (eds) *Sports development: Policy, process and practice.* London: Routledge, pp. 77–117.

King, N. (2009) *Sports policy and governance: Local perspectives.* Oxford, Butterworth-Heinemann.

Lindsey, I. (2006) 'Local partnerships in the United Kingdom for the New Opportunities for PE and Sport programme: A network analysis', *European Sport Management Quarterly* Vol. 6, No. 2: pp. 167–185.

Lindsey, I. (2008) 'Conceptualising sustainability in sports development', *Leisure Studies* Vol. 27, No. 3: pp. 279–294.

Long, J. And Sanderson, I. (2001) 'The social benefits of sport: Where's the proof?', in C. Gratton and I. Henry (eds) *Sport in the city.* London: Routledge, pp. 187–203.

Mackintosh, C. (2008) 'Bonding issues', *Recreation* October 2008: pp. 20–21.

Mackintosh, C. (2011) 'An analysis of County Sports Partnerships in England: The fragility, challenges and complexity of partnership working in sports development', *International Journal of Sports Policy and Politics* Vol. 3, No. 1: pp. 45–64.

Mackintosh, C., Harris, S, and Cutforth, C. (2010) 'European Sports Development Network', *Sports Management* Vol. 14, No. 4: pp. 50–51.

Nichols, G. (2004) 'Crime and punishment and sports development', *Leisure Studies* Vol. 23, No. 2: pp. 177–194.

—— (2007) *Sport and crime reduction: The role of sports in tackling youth crime.* London: Routledge.

Nichols, G., Gratton, C., Shibli, S. and Taylor, P. (2001) 'Local authority support to volunteers in sports clubs', *Managing Leisure* Vol. 3, No. 3: pp. 119–127.

Nichols, G., Taylor, P., James, M., King, L., Holmes, K., and Garrett, R. (2003) 'Pressures on sports volunteers arising from partnerships with central government', *Loisir et Société* Vol. 26, No. 2: pp. 419–430.

Nutley, S. M., Walter, I. and Davies, H.T.O. (2007) *Using evidence: How research can inform public services.* Bristol, The Policy Press.

Pitchford, A. (2005) *Community and sports development research report to Skills Active community development working group.* Gloucester: University of Gloucester.

Robson, S. (2008) 'Partnerships in sport', in K. Hylton and P. Bramham (eds) *Sports development: Policy, process and practice.* London, Routledge, pp. 118–142.

Rowe, N. (2009) 'The Active People Survey: A catalyst for transforming evidence-based sport policy in England', *International journal of sport policy* Vol. 1, No. 1: pp. 89–98.

Sanderson, I. (2002) 'Making sense of "what works": Evidence based policy making as instrumental rationality', *Public Policy Administration* Vol. 17, No. 3: pp. 61–75.

Silverman, D. (2010) *Doing qualitative research*. London: Sage.

Smith, A. and Leech, R. (2010) '"Evidence: What evidence?" Evidence-based policy making and School Sport Partnerships in North West England', *International Journal of Sport Policy* Vol. 2, No. 3: pp. 327–345.

Smith, A. and Waddington, I. (2004) 'Using "Sport in the Community Schemes" to tackle crime and drug use among young people: Some policy issues and problems', *European Physical Education Review* Vol. 10, No. 3: pp. 279–98.

Snape, B. and Binks, P. (2008) 'Re-thinking sport: Physical activity and healthy living among British South Asian Muslim Communities', *Managing Leisure* Vol. 13, No. 1: pp. 23–35.

Sport England (2005) *Strategy of sports research 2005–2008: Towards evidence based decision making in sport*. London: Sport England.

———— (2008) *Sport England strategy 2008–2011*. London: Sport England.

LEADING SPORT FOR DEVELOPMENT? A CASE STUDY ANALYSIS OF THE USE OF GLOBAL NORTH VOLUNTEERS IN SPORT FOR DEVELOPMENT PROGRAMMES IN THE GLOBAL SOUTH

Leona Trimble
University of Central Lancashire

Introduction

As the last decade has demonstrated, sport continues to be used as a tool for social change, particularly on the international stage. The sport for development movement has grown significantly since 2003 when the General Assembly of the United Nations adopted a resolution advocating "sport as a means to promote education, health, development and peace" (United Nations, 2004: p. 1). The understanding and appreciation of the power of sport in contributing to education, health, development and peace within the international community (Beutler, 2008) was further highlighted when the UN declared 2005 to be the International Year of Sport and Physical Education. Thereafter, as Burnett (2010: p. 290) observed, "sport programmes and initiatives were designed, piloted and implemented by a myriad of stakeholders, operating at all levels of society to meaningfully contribute towards achieving the Millennium Development Goals". Of course the sport for development movement is not new, but the rapid expansion of practitioners, scholars, government officials and international working groups who are attempting to sustain the sport for development agenda through integration into domestic and international development policies (Hayhurst, 2009) is becoming increasingly significant. In the last decade the academic research and debate on sport for development has varied in scope and direction. Much attention has been drawn by the impact that sport for development activity has on the global South, with emphasis on human rights (Giulianotti, 2004), gender empowerment (Saavedra, 2009), socially marginalised young people (Crabbe, 2009), young people as

131

peer leaders, and the impact of HIV/AIDS education and leadership programmes (Campbell and McPhail, 2002; Jeanes, 2011; Nicholls, 2009).

Further critical analysis of current sport for development practice points towards a movement that can, through that practice, reinforce aspects of neo-colonialism (Darnell, 2010); is donor-led, can have little meaning to the recipients (Kidd, 2008); and often involves deliverers with a lack of cultural understanding and of local meaning for sport (Guest, 2009). It is within this contextual framework that this paper has been written. It seeks to investigate the merits and limitations of using, in this case, United Kingdom female young leaders to deliver sport for development activities through examining their accounts, reflections and experiences of working in the sport for development arena.

Despite the increasing localization of the sport for development movement and the rising influence of local stakeholders in shaping projects and activity (Lindsey and Gratton, 2011), the majority of work in this area continues to be funded, devised and implemented by 'global north' agencies in conjunction with various volunteers/leaders, also from the global North. However over the last five years there has been considerable progress by NGOs in their practical delivery of sport for development work recruiting 'from within' in addition to the global North volunteers. Peer education and leadership has been increasing used by NGOs to achieve a large majority of sport for development objectives (Nicholls, 2009). This is supported by Jeanes (2011) who argues that young people within the global South are capable of making valuable contributions to sport for development work and should be engaged in consultation. Nicholls (2009: p. 158) stresses that "considerations of power and knowledge centre on concerns that the sport-in-development movement tends to be dominated by a 'vertical hierarchy' which affects donor-recipient and North-South relationships". Whilst there has been some critical examination of the experiences and role of volunteers from the global North in sport for development activities (Darnell, 2007; Guest, 2009), this remains limited. This is despite the huge numbers of volunteers and coaches from the global North who work in sport for development programmes each year and the formalizing of such approaches to development by various international agencies such as UK Sport, Right to Play and the British Council. The purpose of this paper therefore is to:

- examine the experiences of young female leaders from the UK delivering a sport for development initiative in South Africa;

- analyse how such experiences contribute to the development of leadership skills amongst young women from the UK;
- examine the perceived benefits provided by external female leaders working on sport for development projects;
- critically consider the role of external volunteer/leaders within the sport for development movement.

Literature

Women's leadership and empowerment through sport

Many of the United Nations Millennium Development Goals are aimed at changing the position, status and power of women — ensuring universal primary education, promoting gender equality and empowering women and combating HIV/AIDS (Coalter, 2007). Thus a high number of sport for development initiatives focus on women and young girls within a specific cultural context. As Sancar and Sever (2005) have observed, in recent years there has been a notable move in the discourse from requesting 'gender equity in sport', to pushing 'sport for gender equity'. This represents a significant paradigm shift which specifically defines gender equity as an objective in sport for development initiatives, rather than simply promoting the participation of women and girls: "Sport can be a powerful and potentially a radical and transformative tool in empowering girls and women and affecting gender norms and relations throughout a society" (Saavedra, 2009: p. 124). Beutler (2008: p. 365) states that "sport is a powerful cross-cutting tool which can be complementary to existing tools".

The ideals of gender equity, leadership skills and empowerment are inextricably linked and feature heavily in the aims/objectives of many sport for development projects. At the heart of many of these projects, especially those with gender equity as an outcome, is knowledge, understanding, challenging norms and positive reinforcement. Saavedra (2009: p. 125) contends that the relationship between sport and gender is not a universal concept and that any sport for development activity must be "grounded in a clear appreciation of local dynamics". Sport for development must also take into account local understandings of sport, gender, self-esteem and teamwork (Guest, 2009) and the extent to which historical, social and political diversity differentiates meaning of sport and gender in the global North and South. Saavedra (2009) comments that the techniques and perceptions often used to analyse gender and the sport for development movement is dominated and signified by the global North and as such, applies Western values, solutions and norms to a complex situation. In policy making, for example, Hayhurst (2009) comments that often the voice missing from the policy discussions is the sport for development recipient, an omission which impacts on policy formulation, interpretation and delivery. Hayhurst uses the example of gender equity to illustrate this point. He argues that "homogenous international donor policy that is implemented by an NGO will be most likely be imperfectly translated into the experiences and desires of local actors throughout the aid chain" (Hayhurst, 2009: p. 209). This approach to policy making and delivery, particularly in relation to gender relations, fails to account for the historical and local complex contexts.

While there are researchers who postulate that sport has inherent properties that lead to empowerment (Mwaanga, 2003), others including Saavedra (2009) question the use of sport — an arena that is profoundly gendered and dominated by masculine values — for promoting gender equity and empowering young women. Giulianotti (2004) has raised questions about the extent to which 'empowerment' is a clear goal for sport for development projects, particularly within the context of his concerns around donors/recipient dialogue and cross-cultural co-operation. Kabeer (1999: p. 438) defined empowerment as "the power within" which is both an individual as well as a collective process involving all levels of society and structural changes. Mwaanga (2010) further discusses the idea of empowerment at a personal level and urges that not all sports participation automatically leads to personal-level empowerment. On a societal level, the focus of any sport for development project must be embedded within a specific cultural, political, juridical, economic and social setting. Therefore, when considering ideas about gender roles and gender empowerment, the projects must reflect an understanding that gender relations are often deeply engrained in educational systems and social structures (Meier, 2005).

With sport for development projects, then, the focus turns to how the perceptions of empowerment, physical capacities (Mwaanga, 2010) and the development of human capital and collective identities (Lawson, 2005) can be furthered through participation in sport. Here Mwaanga (2010) questions the ability of sport for development projects to move beyond the feeling of empowerment to more significant action which can actually address inequality. The goal of effecting change which strikes at the heart of a society and challenges dominant — often gendered — practices, ideologies, and organizations (Saavedra, 2009) may be best served by focusing on the young people within that society. The role that sport can play in breaking down these barriers, particularly in terms of gender empowerment, is still widely debated. As Saavedra (2009) comments, the dilemma for sport for development projects is that, in sport, male dominance is often asserted over women, gender distinctions and unequal power relations are reinforced, women and girls remain marginalised, and their participation in sport often puts their (perceived) femininity at risk.

In terms of gender equality and power, it is important to review some of the literature regarding the use of football to address these issues. Much has been written about the role of football in sport for development projects. Coalter (2010) comments on the appeal of football being widespread throughout Africa. Armstrong and Giulia-notti (2004) suggest that football can provide one avenue of symbolic mobility for those communities that are denied entry to more conventional forms of social advancement such as education and employment. Meier (2005) suggests that before a program is introduced, a proper communication and information campaign has to be delivered which identifies the local 'gatekeepers' so they can be lobbied to support the development objectives. Saavedra (2009) regards sport as an activity that is profoundly gendered and dominated by masculine values, thus questionable as an arena from which to promote gender equity and empowering young women. Therefore, when using sport, and more specifically football, to work towards gender empowerment and leadership, clearly there are a number of issues to be considered.

On a positive note, the promotion of female sport, the playing of female football in public, could create role models and eventually deconstruct and rearticulate gender norms (Meier, 2005). However the world of sport remains profoundly gendered, with experiences often exclusively male or female, masculine or feminine (Saavedra, 2009). Promoting gender equity through sport has to embrace a holistic gender perspective primarily focusing on the needs of individual human beings and should consciously mix boys and girls for sport activities (if allowed) to offer added value (Meier, 2005). Saavedra (2005) highlights the complex issue of confronting gender and norms of sexuality and discusses how females playing traditionally male games such as football can provide a more direct challenge to male power and wider socio-cultural relations. The notion of challenging gendered norms extends beyond merely participation. For example, females coaching or refereeing boys or mixed-sex groups can get the message across that women have knowledge and leadership skills, but are also capable and familiar with that male-dominated field (Meier, 2005).

Global North volunteers and sport for development

In the last 5 years or so the sport for development work in practice has seen some shift in delivery mechanisms as NGOs train local leaders and educators to deliver key messages through a range of development tools. For example, Right To Play have moved away from a structure focused on global North volunteers to one which has resulted in the hiring and training of 13,000 local leaders and coaches (Right to Play, 2010). These young leaders can then ensure sustainable activities around a range of health, HIV/AIDS and life skills through the training they receive. Coaching for Hope, since 2005, have been training coaches in local communities to deliver football, · HIV awareness and life skills. The UK coaches provide on-going support but the sustainability of the programme rests with the training from within the global South: to date, 700 coaches have been trained (Coaching for Hope, 2010).

That said, sport for development organisations still facilitate much of their activity by using volunteers from the global North to 'improve' the lives of people in the global South. Often this activity reinforces a neo-colonial environment in which the empowered and vocal develop the disempowered and silent (Darnell, 2007). Nicholls (2009: p. 162) draws upon the interconnection between "colonialism, subjugated knowledge and peer education" and how sport in development programmes often lack engagement with young people.

In addition, critical analysis of the use of global North volunteers in sport for development activity has suggested that such individuals are ill-equipped and lack knowledge of local cultural communities (Darnell, 2007; Guest 2009). Placing global North volunteers into unfamiliar contexts to deliver a range of sport for development outcomes is still a major concern for a number of NGOs, despite more delivery being undertaken by global South peer leaders/educators. Kidd (2008) argues that a related issue in this debate is the notion of top-down control, and that so much of sport for development activity is planned and conducted in such a way that many projects may simply impose the values of the global North middle class on the disadvantaged low- and middle-income countries. Guest (2009) observes that global North volunteers are often trained and qualified in sports activity rather than international work or child development. They are therefore frequently unprepared to deal with the complex demands of development work and have little understanding of the potential power and repressive relationships that can exist in their delivery of activities. There are also reports that many non-governmental organisations (NGOs) send inexperienced volunteers without sufficient planning and training into relatively short global South programmes which often are highly popular with donors but make little difference to the recipients (Kidd, 2008). This lack of training for global North volunteers exacerbates an already complex set of factors contextualizing much sport for development work. In particular the lack of understanding of local meaning-making (Guest, 2009), or the failure to hear local voices (Nicholls, 2009), means that inexperienced volunteers find many challenges when undertaking sport for development activity.

Sport for development is clearly a complex and challenging area. Whilst, as illustrated, many projects in the global South are delivered by volunteers from the global North, there are a few studies examining the views of such volunteers on both the benefits they perceive to gain from such experiences but also, and clearly more significantly, what benefits the communities gain from their involvement. This chapter aims to contribute to greater understanding of both the value and limits of global North volunteers within the sport for development movement.

Research context

The research on which this paper draws was carried out during and on return from a two–week 'Women's leadership through football' pilot project initiated and funded by the British Council (BC). The BC approached Coaching for Hope (CfH) for support with the delivery, who in turn approached their charity partner the Football Association (FA) to select the young female footballers who would participate. The project evolved from the BC's Connecting Classrooms programme which was established in 2006. Through such sport programmes the BC aim to "focus on using the inspirational power of sport to build relationships between the UK and countries around the world" (British Council, 2010).

CfH are part of the international volunteering and development charity Skillshare International, and primarily use football as a tool in their aim to reduce poverty, injustice and inequality in the west and south of Africa. They organize courses though which professional coaches from the UK visit African communities to train local youth workers to recognised FA standards, including how to deliver HIV awareness sessions to young people in their communities. CfH staff provide ongoing support to newly qualified South African coaches so that they can develop training initiatives in their own communities (Coaching for Hope, 2010). The 2010 'Women's leadership through football' pilot project thus brought together three organizations that had a tradition of youth leadership and gender equity as illustrated through their respective global projects.

The project was delivered in May 2010 in Johannesburg and Cape Town, South Africa. It involved 12 female young leaders from Birmingham, London and East and North Riding County FAs, four female county development officers, and two female university representatives. The female young leaders were aged between 16 and 19 years and had been selected by their county officers due to their involvement in FA leadership programmes in the UK. The group travelled together to South Africa for a two-week project which incorporated football activity in three schools in Johannesburg and three schools in Cape Town. The activity was designed to promote the full inclusion of girls in mixed football sessions and to train peer educators and teachers on how to deliver mixed football sessions. By using UK female young leaders the aim was to send out a strong message about respecting women playing football and their full and equal inclusion (Coaching for Hope, 2009). The project was arranged with a very short lead-in time of approximately three months once funding had been secured. The timing of the project was designed to gain maximum impact from South Africa hosting the football World Cup in 2010 as part of a wider sport for development agenda on empowering young women through football.

Methods

The methodological approach of this paper was located within an interpretive 'paradigm' which assumes a subjective relationship between researcher and participant (Healy and Perry, 2000). Essentially the aim of the research process was to enable the experiences, perceptions and aspirations of the participants to be heard (Bloxom, 2005) and to inform the paper. Thus a fundamental precept to the methodological approach taken was to allow the respondents' own perspectives to emerge, to explore the ways in which the project was unfolding, how people were working together and to get insight into particular experiences. Throughout the research the emphasis was on experiential accounts of the young UK leaders, encouraging them to consider their expectations and the reality of what they were experiencing. Thus, trying to understand the multiple individual realities experienced within this project led the researcher to adopt a qualitative methodological approach. This approach was designed to be reflective, interactive and challenging (Diamond, 2004) and worthwhile in terms of creating meaningful dialogue to elicit purposeful accounts from the participants (Sharp, 2004).

The relationship-building between the researcher and the participants began during the project itself. During the evenings, the participants were encouraged to work in small groups and reflect on the day's events: challenges, issues, successes and learning points were discussed and recorded by the researcher. This was deemed an essential component of the research process in order to build-up trust between the researcher and the participants who had not met prior to the project, and thus helped to clarify my role as researcher from the outset. Added to this was the completed reflective diaries submitted by four of the girls who were happy for these to be used to inform the research material.

The qualitative data was collected during a post-project evaluation day in July 2010. The 12 young leaders and 3 county FA development officers gathered to debrief and discuss their experiences and to draw out their contrasting narratives. The focus groups were semi-structured with themed areas to discuss within a 30–minute time frame. There were four sessions in total which were designed by CfH and BC. During these discussions the researcher was able to adopt an observational role and record the audio in preparation for transcribing and analysing at a later date. The discussions were facilitated by the CfH and BC staff based on the issues that had arisen during the day. Further qualitative data was collected via 7 semi-structured interviews involving 4 young UK leaders; J (16), J (18), B (18) and R (18) and 3 county development officers; G (24), P (26) and E (27), conducted by the researcher. The focus of the interviews was to gather their views on the use of football in South Africa, the use of young leaders, their experiences in the delivery of the project, and the planning/ preparation prior to embarking on the project. There was also some attention to the lessons learned, particularly of the use of global North volunteers in sport for development activity in South Africa.

This research method was more intrusive and less structured than quantitative research techniques but was regarded as the most appropriate for this study given the exploratory nature of the investigation (Jarratt, 1996). The interviews were conducted sensitively, with conversation allowed to flow naturally by adjusting the pace and style of questions so as to bring out the best in the respondents (Hannabuss, 1996). This strategy also allowed a certain amount of flexibility and it was felt that the researcher was able to capitalise on chance remarks or unexpected events that propelled a new line of investigation (Bryman, 1989). During the interview the researcher made notes on the scripts but also audio recorded the interviews to allow detailed annotation at a later date. The researcher then conducted transcription and analysis which was inductive in nature, allowing the building-up of "a comprehensive picture of ethnographic reality from the respondents' answers" (Hannabuss, 1996: p. 29). A constant comparison-inductive method was used to allow potential categories of meaning to emerge from the data (Hatch, 2002) and through this process the key themes from the research were established.

Findings and analysis

Experiences of UK young female leaders and the development of their leadership skills

During the interviews a key theme emerging was the benefits the young women felt they had gained from their involvement. Participants felt they had increased their confidence, developed their sense of self and generally enjoyed the challenge of delivering activity in different social conditions. B (18) commented:

> I had more confidence. I was more comfortable with what I was saying and it gave me a confidence boost.

Not only did the young leaders comment on their development whilst they were on the project, but their development was noticeable on their return as witnessed by E (27) one of the development officer who observed that:

> Those involved really excelled and their confidence shone. Many of the young women felt their leadership skills had improved. They talked about the experience developing their delivery; they had more ideas and shared with others.

Taking the girls out of their natural coaching environment and out of their comfort zone to challenge their practices was a positive experience, as R (18) said:

> It was an eye-opener; it was different and drastic and has made me more confident.

One of the FA development officers (G, 24), made the following comments on the benefits to the girls of coaching in such challenging context and how this had developed the sporting leadership skills of the girls:

> I saw a tremendous improvement in the leadership qualities of my girls and what was achieved in two weeks in South Africa would take years to achieve here.... It was certainly a test for the young leaders from the UK, which took them out of their comfort zone and meant that they had to think about adapting their practices and drills and ultimately this would develop their leadership skills.

Reflecting on their experiences and the narrative of their involvement in this pilot project, the global North volunteers identified a number of benefits and personal development gains. The consensus was that the project had a significant impact on the development of the leadership skills of the UK girls many of which excelled and their confidence grew as the project progressed. The opportunity presented to the UK young leaders, empowered them and encouraged them to take the lead in the delivery of the sessions. Many of the reflections could be perceived as personal-level empowerment (Mwaanga, 2010) and the use of football in this project was a positive contributing factor. When asked to reflect on what she had achieved for the project, J (18) reflected,

> Coaching the girls, being a leader to them, being a role model for people to look up to...the boys could see me play and say wow that girl can play.

Overall the girls felt that the project helped with their practical coaching skills, improved their confidence, aided their planning, independence and gave them an appreciation of the challenges faced by females in the global South. The experience had a positive effect on the development of the leadership skills for the volunteers/leaders from the global North.

Perceived benefits to the local community

Given the time frame of this project, the identification of benefits to the local community, the South African peer leaders and project participants is likely to be extremely limited and demonstrates one of the key limitations of this and many other sport for development projects. They are frequently not long enough to achieve sustainable impact or change and do not give enough time or attention to robust monitoring of past projects to measure whether they have delivered the outcomes that were intended. Rather naively but not unexpectedly, the hope of the UK females young leaders was that they had made some difference whilst involved in the project. R (18) said:

> It is hard to make an impact in such a short space of time but I think we made an impact on the attitude of the boys and the girls became more confident.

The UK leaders felt that they had provided several relatively intangible benefits to their counterpart South African peer leaders. They talked about raising expectations amongst these girls, 'broadening the minds of the community' more generally, as well as simply promoting the game of women's football and the idea that it is an acceptable game for girls to play. R (18) commented:

> I would like to say that we helped the kids in the schools to get an understanding of what it is like for us coaching and learning [from] them as well and hopefully have an impact on them and trying to get more girls involved in football.

Of course, given the complexities of the issues in the global South and the lack of training and preparation of the young volunteers from the global North for those deep-rooted issues, these perceptions are superficial at best. The potential limit on what they could achieve was a key theme emerging from several of the UK volunteer interviews. J (16) observed that:

> In the schools there were more boys playing than girls, but I think we did make a difference because at the first school we went to there were more girls towards the end of it who had joined in, even if they hadn't played football before, compared to the start when there were only 10.

She reflected further on the limitations of their impact:

> There was some improvement in the numbers in the short time we were there but I don't know if this would continue after we left.

The global North participants also felt their impact was limited not only by the short time they spent in each school but also because of the limited planning and preparation training that had taken place whilst they were still in the UK. J (19) said:

> In terms of the South African girls, they did get involved in the delivery to the boys during the mixed sessions, which gave them confidence that it is acceptable for boys to be coached by girls.

It was clear in most schools that the South African peer leaders did participate in some delivery and did contribute some ideas but it was hard to tell what development might have occurred. It was felt that more encouragement for them to take the lead was required and that more integration between the groups would also have helped. Some observations from the FA development officers regarding the impact on the empowerment of the South African girls highlighted the fact that there was little specific activity directly focused on developing their leadership skills. Nevertheless, there was a sense that some exchanges on new games emerged which could help to develop their leadership skills in the longer term.

In summary therefore, whilst the UK volunteers were able to articulate the numerous benefits they had gained from the project, even within a short space of time, they generally felt these were not balanced to any great extent in their host communities by the project's intended benefits. This might be explained by the fact that, despite having gained the viewpoints of the global North volunteers regarding the perceived benefits to the local community, a limitation in this project has been the absence of local voices. As we have seen, a key element of sport for development activity, as stressed by a number of researchers (Kay, 2009; Nicholls, 2009; Guest, 2009; Saavedra, 2009), is the importance of consultation and listening to local people. In this regard the girls did feel that some sharing of expertise had taken place between themselves and their SA counterparts. They expressed hope that they had planted seeds which over time would grow and flourish. By displaying a confidence which said it was acceptable for girls to play football — the attention they brought, the strong visual presence, the image, the kit — they felt they had sent out a very strong and positive message promoting respect and equality for women playing football. However, the wider ambitious social outcomes of developing gender equity and the empowerment of young women in SA through football were generally not evident. Thus rather than the project not meeting the intended goals, it is more evident that the BC and CfH had set unrealistic goals in the first place, which explains the lack of evidence of such elements in the project outcomes.

Role of external volunteer/leaders within the sport for development movement

Often, one of the criticisms of sport for development work is that projects lack meaningful dialogue with recipient groups, as discussed by Giulianotti (2004). Throughout this project such shortcomings — from the ill-defined roles, to communication and training issues — presented the UK volunteers with significant challenges. P (26) noted that:

More clearly defined roles and responsibilities were needed. Clearer ownership of the different elements of the project was required. Better 'buy in' from the schools would also have helped to achieve outcomes. Overall aim needed to be more clearly defined — what exactly did CfH and the BC want to achieve in such a short space of time?

As the interviews developed it became apparent that limited interaction had occurred between the partnership agencies and key stakeholders at local level, such as teachers and community leaders. This was revealed by a number of the reflections from the participants. J (18) said:

The knowledge in the schools about women and girls football and the project itself was not great, but it depended on the school you went to. Some were a bit like 'well you've just turned up here' kind of thing, they weren't that welcoming.

Such reactions surprised the girls as they had expected the teachers, girls and everyone in the schools to know why they were there and what the goals of the project were. But indifference and lack of knowledge was not something that the UK girls expected or were used to.

However, the local reactions are not surprising given the lack of engagement or communication with the schools and teachers in the planning stages and the somewhat imposed activity upon the recipients by the donors (Kidd,2008). It was evident that despite involvement in the BCs Connecting Classrooms' programme the global South 'gatekeepers' (Meier, 2005) in this pilot project had not been involved in enough meaningful communication regarding the objectives and implementation. Feedback from the development officers also reinforced the problems with this approach in relation to lack of knowledge, 'buy-in' and resistance from some of the schools that the UK leaders visited. The officers repeatedly stressed the need for meaningful and continual dialogue between all of the organisations, but particularly the recipients at local level during the planning stages where the activity was taking place. The FA development officers in particular felt that more preparation was needed beforehand in South Africa. G (24) commented that:

We really needed to be working with the right girls from the right classes who had been clearly identified beforehand and [with whom] some preparation work had been done.

These reflections and observations further reflect the often criticized practice of many sport for development projects. As P (26) observed:

> It felt a bit like we didn't really take into consideration what their needs were and what they wanted out of the project.

Further critical analysis of this project, based upon the observations of the UK volunteers, highlights its alignment with the neo-colonial tendencies of the wider sport for development movement and the donor led approach which (Kidd, 2008) articulates. The fact that this came across so clearly from the UK girls themselves suggests that they were not oblivious to this aspect of the project, which was essentially imported by and managed from the global North (Darnell, 2007). The schools were selected due to their involvement in Connecting Classrooms, but in practice it is unclear the extent to which the SA schools wanted or benefited from this project. This supports Giulianotti (2004) who calls for more dialogue between the donors and recipients before sports-related aid is offered in order that the recipients are sufficiently empowered to claim ownership over the projects. As E (27) noted:

> More preparation beforehand in South Africa... [was required], more encouragement for them to take the lead. It was too easy for the UK girls to take over. The South African schools needed more preparation for our arrival in order to make it worthwhile and to make a difference.

There is no doubt that the sharing of experiences through football between the UK volunteers and the South African peer leaders was enjoyable and fun, but the top-down approach adopted on this project clearly illustrates the imbalance between the empowered and disempowered (Darnell, 2007).

The limited critical analysis of the use of global North volunteers in sport for development activity repeatedly suggests that they are too ill-equipped and lacking in knowledge of local cultural communities (Darnell, 2007; Guest, 2009) to be effective at achieving the broader social outcomes they are tasked with. This was also reflected in the UK reflective accounts, as E (27), one of the female development officers made the following observation:

> Some of the younger girls were aged only 16 [and] it was quite a test [for them] to be away from home to a developing country at such a young age. This was particularly [so] because of the lack of awareness or education beforehand.

Despite the challenges they were likely to face and the continued emphasis within development work of volunteers having some knowledge and understanding of local context, these young women had received limited information before travelling on the types of conditions to expect. They were largely unaware of the prevalent social conditions and how the gender equity and empowerment objectives that they were expected to achieve were contextualized within the broader social arena in which that they would be delivering. Placing young volunteers in unfamiliar context to deliver a range of sport for development outcomes is not uncommon. One of the key questions to be asked therefore is how well prepared the UK young female leaders were to deliver a sport for development project of this nature in South Africa. The experiences of volunteers on this project would suggest they were not well equipped at all. From the outset it appeared clear to the UK volunteers that that planning and preparation was limited. J (19) said:

> There was a lack of training beforehand, particularly about the HIV/Aids issues and problems. We needed more preparation and briefing about the country and its culture so there could be a greater understanding of the cultural barriers. There was a lot to take in, in such a short space of time.

Overall, the girls felt that the project had significant shortcomings in planning and implementation. Lack of communication, coupled with lack of training for both the SA leaders and themselves, conspired to facilitate a donor-led project of which it was difficult for host schools and local community to see the relevance. A substantial element of this project failed in practice to take account of local voices (Kay, 2009) or to consider the local meaning for sport (Guest, 2009) for the SA young leaders or participants. At a practical level the UK volunteers were ill-equipped to deliver activity at a broader level, and their experiences can be seen as symptomatic of what Kidd (2008) describes as the top-down control prevalent within so many sport for development projects. There is an assumption that even ill-equipped UK leaders still have considerable expertise to 'bestow' on the local communities, but in doing so they are exhibiting and reproducing the neo-colonial effects of global North initiated and managed projects.

Conclusion

Overall, the merits of this pilot sport for development project appear to be UK-centric in terms of improved practical coaching skills, improved confidence, planning, independence and an appreciation of the challenges faced by females in the global South. Whilst the UK volunteers were able to articulate the numerous benefits they gained from the project, even within a short space of time they generally felt similar benefits had not been gained to any great extent by their counterparts in the host communities. Given the short duration of this project again this is hardly surprising, but it raises questions about the unrealistic objectives for this project and what the British Council and Coaching for Hope wanted to achieve. The perceived benefits to the global South leaders appeared to be extremely limited — some shared ideas and experiences and the opportunity to lead mixed football sessions. But these were not reflective of the broader 'lofty promises' that the project aimed to deliver. The construction of the project points towards an approach reflecting neo-colonial tendencies (Darnell, 2010), with a global North-defined problem, and a donor-led solution using ill-equipped global North volunteers with limited training. As Guest (2009) suggests, sport for development projects are well intentioned and have noble desired outcomes, but have many shortcomings in practice. The experience of this project had a positive effect on the development of the leadership skills for the volunteers/leaders from the global North, but the wider ambitious social outcomes of developing gender equity and empowerment of young women in SA through football were generally not in evidence.

Whilst this paper has largely been critical of the current conditions that prevail in the use of global North volunteers it is not the intention to suggest they cannot provide any value to the sport for development movement. However if this is to occur, global North volunteers need to support a locally-led, community-shaped project, not being the deliverers of an externally-constructed, top-down, imposed approach. They have to be appropriately trained and sensitized to the broader cultural, social and political contexts of the communities in which they will be working. An encouraging aspect emerging from the interviews in this research was the recognition by the UK volunteers that they were making a limited impact on their host communities. They readily problematised their lack of experience and training in the broader sport for development agenda and were critical of and realistic about what they did and did not achieve, and the reasons why. They were in agreement that it was naive and simplistic to think that UK sports volunteers could effectively undertake sport for development work of this nature with limited training or preparation. They also recognised the need to move away from a neo-colonialist approach to sport for development and instead engage from the outset with local partners and particularly recipient communities about what the issues are at local level, about how sport may be used to challenge and improve these issues, and what is the best and most appropriate delivery method. This would suggest that practitioners within the sport for development movement are becoming increasingly aware of and sensitive to the criticisms being leveled at the wider movement, although as yet systemic changes to address them is not obviously occurring.

Finally, the limitations of the paper are recognized. Whilst offering a critical analysis of the use of global North volunteers, it would have been valuable to add weight to this by gaining the views of local participants and leaders, and particularly key stakeholders within the schools. Such analysis would likely provide more detailed insights to assist with analysing the limitations of the project. But it could also provide greater clarity on how sport could be more effectively used by international stakeholders to create meaningful impact within local communities in the global South.

Acknowledgements

I am grateful for the patience and support shown by the LSA editorial team. I am indebted to Dr Ruth Jeanes for her insightful comments, feedback and encouragement which transformed this paper.

References

Beutler, I. (2008) 'Sport serving development and peace: Achieving the goals of the United Nations through sport', *Sport in Society* Vol. 11, No. 4: pp. 359–369.

Bloxom, J. (2005) 'Moving from the margins', *ARVAC Bulletin*, No. 96: pp. 7–8.

British Council (2010) 'Connecting classrooms', available from http: // www.britishcouncil.org/learning-connecting-classrooms.htm. [accessed 30 November 2010].

Bryman, A. (1989)'*Research methods and organizational studies*. London: Routledge.

Burnett, C. (2010) 'Sport-for-development approaches in the South African context: A case study analysis', *South African Journal for Research in Sport, Physical Education and Recreation*, Vol. 32, No. 1: pp. 29–42.

Campbell, C. and McPhail, C. (2002) 'Peer education, gender and the development of critical consciousness: participatory HIV prevention by South African youth', *Social Science and Medicine* Vol. 55, No. 2: pp. 331–345.

Crabbe, T. (2009) 'Getting to know you: Using sport to engage and build relationships with socially marginalized young people', in R. Levermore and A. Beacom (eds) *Sport in International Development*. London: Palgrave Macmillan, pp: 176–197.

Coaching for Hope (2009) *Coach training course: Limited resource football coaching courses*. York: Coaching for Hope.

—— (2010) available from http: //www.coachingforhope. org/about_us. php [accessed 30 November 2010]

Coalter, F. (2007) *A wider role for sport: Who's keeping the score?*'London: Routledge.

—— (2010) 'Sport-for-development: Going beyond the boundary?', *Sport in Society* Vol. 13, No. 9: pp. 1374–1391.

Darnell, S. C. (2007) 'Playing with Race: *Right to Play* and the production of Whiteness in "Development through sport", *Sport in Society* Vol. 10, No. 4: pp. 61–87.

—— (2010) 'Power politics and sport-for-development and peace: Investigating the utility of sport for international development', *Sociology of Sport* Vol. 27, No. 1: pp. 54–75.

Diamond, J. (2004) 'Local regeneration initiatives and capacity building: Whose "capacity" and""building" for what?', *Community Development Journal* Vol. 39, No. 2: pp. 177–189.

Giulianotti, R. (2004) 'Human rights, globalization and sentimental education: The case of sport', *Sport in Society* Vol. 7, No. 3: pp. 355–369.

Guest, A. M. (2009) 'The diffusion of development-through-sport: Analyzing the history and practice of the Olympic Movement's grassroots outreach to Africa"*Sport in Society* Vol. 12, No. 10: pp. 1336–1352.

Hatch, J. A. (2002) *Doing qualitative research in education settings*. Albany: State University of New York Press.

Hayhurst, L.M.C (2009) 'The power to shape policy: Charting sport for development and peace policy discourses', *International Journal of Sport Policy* Vol. 1, No. 2: pp. 203–227.

Hannabuss, S. (1996) 'Research interviews', *New Library World* Vol. 97, No. 1129: pp. 22–30.

Healy, M. and Perry, C. (2000) 'Comprehensive criteria to judge validity and reliability of qualitative research within the realism paradigm', *Qualitative Market Research — An International Journal* Vol. 3, No. 3: pp. 118–126.

Jarratt, D. (1996) 'A comparison of two alternative interviewing techniques used within an integrated research design: A case study in outshopping using semi-structured and non-directed interviewing techniques', *Marketing Intelligence & Planning* Vol. 14, No. 6: pp. 6–15.

Jeanes, R. (2011) 'Education through sport? Examining HIV/AIDS education and sport-for-development through the perspectives of Zambian young people', *Sport, Education and Society* iFirst article, pp. 1–19.

Kay, T. (2009) 'Developing through sport: Evidencing sport impacts on young people', *Sport in Society* Vol. 12, No. 5: pp. 1177–1191.

Kabeer, N. (1999) 'Resources, agency, achievements: Reflections on the measurement of women's empowerment', *Development and Change* Vol. 30, No. 3: pp. 435–464.

Kidd, B. (2008) 'A new social movement: Sport for development and peace', *Sport in Society* Vol. 11, No. 4: pp. 370–380.

Lawson, H.A. (2005) 'Empowering people, facilitating community development and contributing to sustainable development: The social work of sport, exercise, and physical education programmes', *Education & Society* Vol. 1, No. 1: pp. 135–160.

Lindsey, I. and Gratton, A. (2011) 'An "international movement"? De-centring sport-for-development within Zambian communities', *International Journal of Sport Policy and Politics* DOI:10.1080/ 19406940.2011.627360

Meier, M. (2005) *Gender equity, sport and development.* Swiss Academy for Development. Boezingenstrasse: SAD.

Mwaanga, O. (2003) 'HIV/AIDS at risk adolescent girls empowerment through participation in top level football and Edusport in Zambia', *Sport and Exercise Psychology Masters thesis*, Oslo: Norwegian University of Sport and Physical Education.

—— (2010) 'Sport for addressing HIV/AIDS: Explaining our convictions', *LSA Newsletter* No. 85 (March). Eastbourne: Leisure Studies Association, pp. 58–64.

Nicholls, S. (2009) 'On the backs of peer educators: Using theory to interro-gate the role of young people in the field of sport-in-development', in R. Levermore and A. Beacom (eds) *Sport in international develop-ment.* London: Palgrave Macmillan, pp: 156–175.

Right to Play (2010) *Annual Report.* Available from http://www. right toplay.com/canada/news-and-media/PublishingImages/Annual-Report-2010-1.jpg [accessed 12 December 2011]

Saavedra, M. (2005) *Women, sport and development.* Available from: http://www.sportandev.org/data/document/document/148.pdf [accessed 1 November 2010].

—— (2009) 'Dilemma and opportunities in gender and sport-in-devel-opment', in R. Levermore and A. Beacom (eds) *Sport in International Development.* London: Palgrave Macmillan, pp: 124–155.

Sancar, A. and Sever, C. (2005) 'Sport and gender', in *Sport for Development and Peace.* Switzerland: Agency for Development and Cooperation, pp. 1–15.

Sharp, C. (2004) 'Developing outcome indicators', *ARVAC Bulletin* No. 92: pp. 5–6.

United Nations (2004) 'Sport as a means to promote education, health, development and peace', *General Assembly Resolution 58/5.* New York: United Nations.

Leisure Studies Association

LSA Publications

LSA

An extensive list of publications on a wide range of leisure studies topics, produced by the Leisure Studies Association since the late 1970s, is available from LSA Publications.

A number of LSA volumes are detailed on the following pages, and full information may be obtained on older, newer and forthcoming LSA volumes from:

LSA Publications, c/o M. McFee
The Chelsea School, University of Brighton
Eastbourne BN20 7SP (UK)
email: myrene.mcfee@leisure-studies-association.info

Among other benefits, members of the Leisure Studies Association may purchase LSA Publications at preferential rates. Please contact LSA at the above address for information regarding membership of the Association, LSA Conferences, and LSA Newsletters.

ONLINE

Complete information about LSA Publications:

www.leisure-studies-association.info/LSAWEB/Publications.html

IDENTITIES, CULTURES AND VOICES IN LEISURE AND SPORT

**LSA Publication No. 116.   ISBN 978 1 905369 27 0   [2011]
eds. Beccy Watson and Julie Harpin**

Contents

DELIVERING EQUALITY IN SPORT AND LEISURE

LSA Publication No. 115.   ISBN 978 1 905369 26 3   [2011]
eds. Jonathan Long, Hayley Fitzgerald and Pete Millward

Contents

COMMUNITY AND INCLUSION IN LEISURE RESEARCH AND SPORT DEVELOPMENT

**LSA Publication No. 114. ISBN 978 1 905369 25 6 [2011]
eds. Aarti Ratna and Brett Lashua**

Contents

CHILDREN, YOUTH AND LEISURE

LSA Publication No. 113. ISBN 978 1 905369 24 5 [2011]
eds. Ruth Jeanes and Jonathan Magee

Contents

RECORDING LEISURE LIVES: HOLIDAYS AND TOURISM IN 20TH CENTURY BRITAIN

LSA Publication No. 112.   ISBN 978 1 905369 23 2   [2011]
eds. Bob Snape and Daniel Smith

Contents

WELLBEING, HEALTH AND LEISURE

LSA Publication No. 111. ISBN 978 1 905369 22 5 [2010]
eds. Ian Wellard and Mike Weed

Contents

LEISURE IDENTITIES AND AUTHENTICITY

LSA Publication No. 110.   ISBN 978 1 905369 21 8   [2010]
ed. Louise Mansfield and Dikaia Chatziefstathiou

Contents

LEISURE EXPERIENCES: SPACE, PLACE AND PERFORMANCE

**LSA Publication No. 109.   ISBN 978 1 905369 20 1   [2010]
eds. Marion Stuart Hoyle and Jane Lovell**

Contents

THIRD AGE AND LEISURE RESEARCH: PRINCIPLES AND PRACTICE

LSA Publication No. 108. ISBN 978 1 905369 19 5 [2010]
ed. Barbara Humberstone

Contents

RECORDING LEISURE LIVES: SPORTS, GAMES AND PASTIMES IN 20TH CENTURY BRITAIN

LSA Publication No. 107.   ISBN 978 1 905369 18 8   [2010]
eds. Bob Snape and Helen Pussard

Contents

LEISURE AND TOURISM: INTERNATIONAL PERSPECTIVES ON CULTURAL PRACTICE

LSA Publication No. 106.   ISBN 978 1 905369 17 1   [2009]
ed. Scott Fleming with **Hazel Andrews, Peter Hackett, Mark Meadows, Martin Selby**

Contents

TOURISM AND LEISURE: LOCAL COMMUNITIES AND LOCAL CULTURES IN THE UK

LSA Publication No. 105. ISBN 978 1 905369 16 4 [2009]
ed. Jayne Caudwell, with Hazel Andrews, Peter Hackett, Mark Meadows, Martin Selby

Contents

ON THE EDGE: LEISURE, CONSUMPTION AND THE REPRESENTATION OF ADVENTURE SPORTS

**LSA Publication No. 104. ISBN 978 1 905369 15 7 [2009]
eds. Joan Ormrod and Belinda Wheaton**

Contents

RECORDING LEISURE LIVES: HISTORIES, ARCHIVES AND MEMORIES OF LEISURE IN 20TH CENTURY BRITAIN

LSA Publication No. 103.   ISBN 978 1 905369 13 3   [2008]
eds. Bob Snape and Helen Pussard

Contents

WHATEVER HAPPENED TO THE LEISURE SOCIETY? THEORY, DEBATE AND POLICY

LSA Publication No. 102.   ISBN 978 1 905369 13 3   [2008]
eds. Paul Gilchrist and Belinda Wheaton

Contents

RELOCATING THE LEISURE SOCIETY: MEDIA, CONSUMPTION AND SPACES

LSA Publication No. 101. ISBN 978 1 905369 12 6 [2008]
eds. Jayne Caudwell, Steve Redhead, Alan Tomlinson

Contents

SPORT, LEISURE, CULTURE AND SOCIAL CAPITAL: DISCOURSE AND PRACTICE

LSA Publication No. 100. ISBN 978 1 905369 11 9 [2008]
eds. Mike Collins, Kirsten Holmes, Alix Slater

Contents

MAKING SPACE: MANAGING RESOURCES FOR LEISURE AND TOURISM

LSA Publication No. 99. ISBN 978 1 905369 10 2 [2007]
eds. Tim Gale, Jenny Hill and Nigel Curry

Contents

SOCIAL AND CULTURAL CHANGE: MAKING SPACE(S) FOR LEISURE AND TOURISM

LSA Publication No. 98.   ISBN 978 1 905369 09 6   [2007]
eds. Maria Casado-Diaz, Sally Everett and Julie Wilson

Contents

URBAN TRANSFORMATIONS: REGENERATION AND RENEWAL IN LEISURE AND TOURISM

LSA Publication No. 96.   ISBN 978 1 905369 00   [2007]
eds. Cara Aitchison, Greg Richards and Andrew Tallon

Contents

FESTIVALS AND EVENTS: CULTURE AND IDENTITY IN LEISURE, SPORT AND TOURISM

LSA Publication No. 94.   ISBN 978 1 905369 05 8 [2007]
eds. Cara Aitchison and Annette Pritchard

Contents

EVENTS AND FESTIVALS:
EDUCATION, IMPACTS AND EXPERIENCES

LSA Publication No. 93. ISBN 978 1 905369 04 1 [2006]
eds. Scott Fleming and Fiona Jordan

Contents

CASE STUDIES IN EVENT MARKETING AND CULTURAL TOURISM

LSA Publication No. 92. ISBN: 978 1 905369 03 4 [2006]
eds. Jane Ali-Knight and Donna Chambers

Contents

ETHICAL ISSUES IN LEISURE RESEARCH

LSA Publication No. 90. ISBN 978 1 905369 01 0 [2006]
eds. Scott Fleming and Fiona Jordan

Contents

EVALUATING SPORT AND ACTIVE LEISURE FOR YOUNG PEOPLE

LSA Publication No. 88.   ISBN: 0 906337 99 2 [2005] pp. 236+xviii
eds. Kevyn Hylton, Anne Flintoff and Jonathan Long

Contents

LEISURE, SPACE AND VISUAL CULTURE: PRACTICES AND MEANINGS

**LSA Publication No. 84. ISBN: 0 906337 95 X [2004] pp. 292+xxii
eds. Cara Aitchison and Helen Pussard**

Contents

LEISURE, MEDIA AND VISUAL CULTURE: REPRESENTATIONS AND CONTESTATIONS

**LSA Publication No. 83. ISBN: 0 906337 94 1 [2004] pp. 282
eds. Cara Aitchison and Helen Pussard**

Contents

ACCESS AND INCLUSION IN LEISURE AND TOURISM

LSA Publication No. 81. ISBN: 0 906337 92 5 [2003] pp. 288
eds. Bob Snape, Edwin Thwaites, Christine Williams

Contents

LEISURE STUDIES:
TRENDS IN THEORY AND RESEARCH

LSA Publication No. 77. ISBN: 0 906337 88 7 [2001] pp. 198 + iv
eds. Stan Parker and Lesley Lawrence

Contents

LEISURE CULTURES, CONSUMPTION AND COMMODIFICATION

LSA Publication No. 74. ISBN: 0 906337 85 2 [2001] pp. 158+xi
ed. John Horne

Contents

LEISURE AND SOCIAL INCLUSION: NEW CHALLENGES FOR POLICY AND PROVISION

**LSA Publication No. 73. ISBN: 0 906337 84 4 [2001] pp. 204
eds. Gayle McPherson and Malcolm Reid**

Contents

HER OUTDOORS: RISK, CHALLENGE AND ADVENTURE IN GENDERED OPEN SPACES

LSA Publication No. 66 [1999] ISBN: 0 906337 76 3; pp. 131
Edited by Barbara Humberstone

Contents

POLICY AND PUBLICS

LSA Publication No. 65. ISBN: 0 906337 75 5 [1999] pp. 167
Edited by Peter Bramham and Wilf Murphy

Contents

LEISURE, TOURISM AND ENVIRONMENT (II) PARTICIPATION, PERCEPTIONS AND PREFERENCES

LSA Publication No. 50 (Part II) ISBN: 0 906337 69 0; pp. 177+xii
Edited by Malcolm Foley, Matt Frew and Gayle McPherson

Contents